FOR A TIME WE CANNOT SEE

FOR A TIME WE CANNOT SEE

LIVING TODAY IN LIGHT *of* HEAVEN

CRAWFORD LORITTS

MOODY PUBLISHERS
CHICAGO

All Scripture quotations, unless otherwise indicated, are taken from the *New American Standard Bible®*, Copyright © The Lockman Foundation 1960, 1962, 1963, 1968, 1971, 1972, 1973, 1975, 1977. Used by permission.

Scripture quotations marked NASB are taken from the *New American Standard Bible®*, Copyright © The Lockman Foundation 1960, 1962, 1963, 1968, 1971, 1972, 1973, 1975, 1977, 1995. Used by permission.

All italics used in Scripture quotations are added by the author for emphasis.

Library of Congress Cataloging-in-Publication Data

Loritts, Crawford W.
    For a time we cannot see : living today in light of heaven / Crawford W. Loritts, Jr.
        p. cm.
    Includes bibliographical references.
    ISBN-13: 978-0-8024-5525-3
    1. Christian life. I. Title.

BV4501.3.L665 2005
248.4—dc22

                                                    2005009858

ISBN: 0-8024-5525-5
ISBN-13: 978-0-8024-5525-3

1 3 5 7 9 10 8 6 4 2

Printed in the United States of America

For:
Brian, David, Darryl, Benjamin, Kevin, and André
Our journey has reminded me that we are living for a time we cannot see!

Contents

	Acknowledgments	8
Introduction:	That Subtle Longing	11
Chapter One:	Live in the Light of the Cross	21
Chapter Two:	Keep Your Eyes on the Prize	33
Chapter Three:	Letting God Lead Your Life	47
Chapter Four:	Stay in the Moment	61
Chapter Five:	Be Fervent	75
Chapter Six:	Spiritual Footprints	91
Chapter Seven:	Live the Truth	107
Chapter Eight:	Get Ready	121
Chapter Nine:	Hold On!	135
	Notes	149

Acknowledgments

The books I have written have been a team effort, and this one is no exception.

Our children are adults now. Karen and I are full of gratitude to God for what He is doing in their lives. We are seeing the "fruit" of their choices and decisions. They have developed their own walks and relationships with the Lord, and we feel honored and privileged to have been used by God to contribute to their spiritual foundation and to launch them to a time we cannot see. Thank you Bryan, Heather, Bryndan, and Holly. You all are the primary reasons why I have written this book.

In recent years I have had the joy of mentoring some emerging leaders. In many respects, I have received far more than I have given. This has been one of the most rewarding experiences of all my years in ministry. As a result of my journey with these men, I have come to grips in a deeper way with the implications of eternity in regard to how we should approach and live the Christian life. They have taught me to value what we cannot immediately measure. Thank you, brothers, for reminding me of the motivation of heaven.

My wife, Karen, is my life-partner and best friend. We have been married for more than thirty-four years. Her consistent walk with the Lord, her desire to obey Him in all things, and her serving, self-sacrificing spirit toward others serves as a loving source of accountability for me. Her life exhibits the values of eternity. Thank you, sweetheart, for your compelling example of what I have tried to write about in this book. I love you more today than ever before!

Dave Boehi, you are a lifesaver! Dave came alongside me and helped me to shape the thoughts and approach to this book. His insights and skill as a writer proved to be invaluable. It was a joy to work with you.

This is now my fifth book with Moody Publishers. They are a class act! Your heart for ministry and your desire to see lives transformed through the printed page is evident in how you steward the message on the author's heart. Greg Thorton, Bill Thrasher, Betsey Newenhuyse, Ali Childers, and Pam Pugh are friends and colleagues who have helped to expand the influence of my ministry for the honor and glory of God. Thank you.

Leonard ("Scottie") Scott is my executive assistant. Scottie, thank you for all that you do to help me to stay on task. Your friendship and the professional, gracious way you approach your responsibilities gives me great confidence and freedom to minister without distraction. And I certainly needed that freedom as I wrote this book!

Linda Waugh manages our website and handles a host of other responsibilities. Not only is she incredibly competent, she has amazing capacity to get things done. Thank you, Linda, for your part in easing the load so that I can focus on what is on my heart. It would have been very difficult to write this book without you!

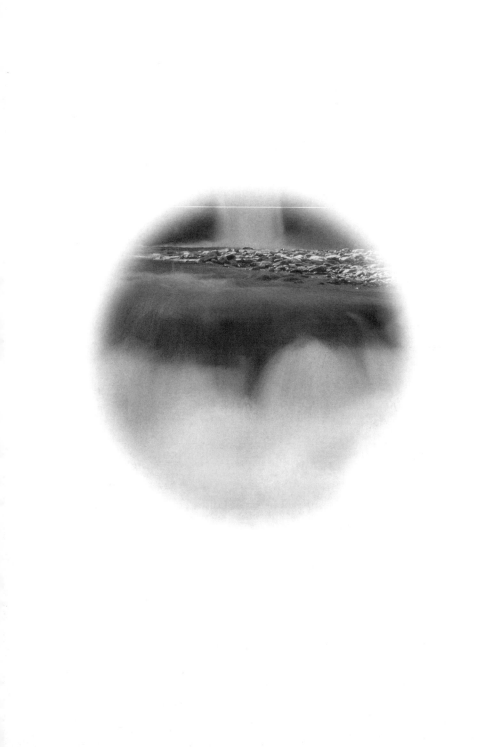

That
Subtle
Longing

We've all felt it.

Perhaps you felt it as a college student as you studied for final exams and looked forward to Christmas at home with your family . . . or as a soldier in a foreign land, dreaming of returning home to your loved ones . . . or as a traveler on a stormy night, with thunder and lightning crashing around you, only wanting to return to the warmth, safety, and dryness of your home.

I know the feeling, the longing. For more than thirty years now, I have traveled around the country and around the world, speaking in distant places far away from those who mean so very much to me. I realize that God has called me to this ministry, and that means I must be faithful in fulfilling that call. And I love what I do. I'm humbled by what God so graciously does through me. There is great joy as I see lives changed in these various places I travel to and share His Word.

But no matter what city or distant country I may be in, or how encouraging or thrilling the ministry may be, I carry with me a longing to be home. That longing is my travel companion. In fact, I *enjoy* its company, because longing reminds me that, in a very real sense, I belong to some very special people who love me and believe in me.

This yearning reminds me that although I am on a journey with a mission, there is a place where I belong, and it's called *home.* While I am away, longing keeps in check my choices and decisions. It helps me to live and behave in such a way that I won't betray the trust and confidence of those who are at home waiting for my return. In fact, longing helps me to stay in touch while I am away. It forces me to make communication with home a priority. Longing reminds me that home is both my destiny and my identity.

But there's another, subtler longing we can sense in our quieter moments. It can sneak up on us, a sense of . . . incompletion, of something missing. This yearning is similar to my longing for home when I travel, or to the soldier's longing for home when he is in harm's way overseas. Yet the feeling is much deeper. We long, no, we *yearn,* for our eternal home, even if we don't realize it.

We feel an emptiness in our lives, so we try to fill it by pursuing career or accomplishment or adventure or possessions or entertainment or relationships—and nothing works. With each effort we inevitably feel that familiar sense of dissatisfaction and restlessness.

Those of us who are followers of Christ need to be reminded that there is a place that is really ours—a home we were created for. God has given us the gift of eternal life, and He has placed the longing for heaven in our hearts. This is our home, our destiny, and our calling.

WRITTEN IN OUR HEARTS

Although heaven is often mentioned in the Bible, it's difficult to form a clear picture of what it will be like. In the Scriptures, heaven is described more than it is explained. We are left with a sense of mystery that piques our interest and fuels our anticipation. Here's a partial list, describing our destiny:

The Bible tells us, for example, that heaven is where God dwells (1 Kings 8:22–23, 30; Isaiah 66:1). In that dwelling place, God first thought of us and formed us (Psalm 139:13; Ephesians 3:15). Heaven is the residence of angelic beings (Matthew 18:10). It is our Savior's residence (Mark 16:19; Acts 1:9–11) and a place of endless worship (Isaiah 6:1–3; Revelation 4).

Heaven is where we will be rewarded (Matthew 5:12). It is a place of justice and impartiality (Ephesians 6:9). It is the place of our inheritance (1 Peter 1:4). Heaven is our origin (Ephesians 3:15) and the destiny of every follower of Christ (John 14:1–3; 2 Corinthians 5:1–8).

Philippians 3:20 tells us, "For our citizenship is in heaven, from which also we eagerly wait for a Savior, the Lord Jesus Christ." We will not see heaven until we die, but the Bible teaches that the longing for heaven is a dominant motivation for living the Christian life. This calling and longing is written in the heart of every true follower of Christ.

REACTION OR INTENTION?

And yet, often, we don't live like we believe it. We live fragmented, hurried lives, wrapped up in the present and devoid of overarching purpose and perspective. We build impressive resumes and raise our kids to be achievers, but in the midst of all this activity and affluence, there's an emptiness, like the hole in the middle of a doughnut. We spend too much and reflect too little. We live by reaction rather than by intention, bouncing from crisis to crisis without stepping back and listening to those longings we keep pushing down.

And then there are the voices of the culture, offering enticing definitions of who and what we ought to be and do. Would-be counselors offer appealing, but dead-end, solutions to life's dilemmas. Advertising tells us where we ought to live, what we ought to drive, where we ought to eat, and what we ought to wear. Music, television, and the movies have become the prophets and preachers in our lives, delivering compelling messages that we sometimes unknowingly incorporate into our worldview—for better and for worse.

For example, we have created and packaged a theology that not only sanitizes but also justifies raw materialism. It's popularly known as the "prosperity gospel." The prophets of this gospel declare it is our right and calling to be wealthy, and they flaunt their ostentatious lifestyles as the fruit of godliness.

Now riches and well-being are indeed gifts from God. But nowhere in the Scriptures are we taught that wealth is our right as followers of Jesus Christ. This teaching violates the purity and integrity of the gospel. This is an attempt to manipulate God to endorse materialism by using "faith" as a means to demand that He give us what we want. We're left with a Christianity that mirrors the self-centered values of our culture without offering a biblical, supernatural alternative. This gives us permission to live as if this life is the final pay-off. The longing for our ultimate destiny has been traded in for square footage down here.

But rather than living for the present, we should be living for a time we cannot see.

"WELCOME HOME"

I would challenge you to surrender to the call of heaven. This destiny provides meaning and significance.

Have you seen the movie *Antwan Fisher?* This film tells the moving story of a young man who struggles with anger and pain because of the abuse he experienced growing up in a foster home. He feels disconnected because he doesn't know his family. His deepest desire is for family, to know to whom he belongs, to have a home.

While serving in the navy, Antwan is encouraged to find his family by a navy psychologist (played by Denzel Washington), who serves as a mentor and father figure in his life. With bits and pieces of information, Antwan heads out on his search, and he is successful. He learns his father is dead but meets his father's family. Then an uncle takes him to meet his mother.

As he enters the apartment of the woman who gave birth to him in prison, he is filled with anticipation and hope that this is going to be a joyful reunion. But it's not. She sits there, not knowing how to respond. It's as if she's in shock. The meeting is a disappointment.

Disappointed and once again rejected, Antwan returns to the home of his aunt. He walks through the door, and to his surprise he finds a room full of people—his extended family that has gathered to meet him. He is swallowed up in a sea of love and acceptance. And when he walks into the dining room, there is an enormous feast, a banquet in his honor. His grandmother, the matriarch of the family, says, "Welcome home."

As we live the Christian life, we must embrace the tension of both living this life to its fullest down here and at the same time understanding that this is not our home. We are pilgrims on a journey to our real home, where there is a family and a banquet waiting for us, and a Savior eager to say, "Welcome home."

PURPOSE, PASSION, PERSPECTIVE

The apostle Paul points us to the perspective and the motivation that should anchor us on our journey. Read carefully these words from I Corinthians 3:10–15. Weigh them. Let your mind absorb them.

> *According to the grace of God which was given to me, as a wise master builder I laid a foundation, and another is building upon it. But let each man be careful how he builds upon it. For no man can lay a foundation other than the one which is laid, which is Jesus Christ. Now if any man builds upon the foundation with gold, silver, precious stones, wood, hay, straw, each man's work will become evident; for the day will show it, because it is to be revealed with fire; and the fire itself will test the quality of each man's work. If any man's work which he has built upon it remains, he shall receive a reward. If any man's work is burned up, he shall suffer loss; but he himself shall be saved, yet so as through fire.*

There are four observations I want to make based on this passage. First, *the foundation of our lives is Jesus Christ* (v. 11). The Christian life is the life of Christ living in and through us. Jesus Christ should be everything to us. He is our reason for living, and as our foundation, He brings strength and stability to the structure of our lives.

Second, *we must approach life with discernment and great care because our lives reflect the foundation upon which we are built* (vv. 10–11). Every time we trade in the motivation of responding to God's love and provision for the stuff of this life, we introduce foreign substances to our foundation. It weakens the building (our lives) and cheapens the structure.

When our house was built years ago, the builder did not dig the foundation for the chimney deep enough. After a few years, it began to pull away from the house. It was supposedly fixed, but not for long. The chimney once again developed cracks and pulled away from the house. We discovered that the contractor had left some of the old bricks and mortar inside the chimney! The stuff didn't belong there. There was too much weight, and it caused damage to the structure.

Some of us have absorbed the "foreign substances" of this life. It weighs us down and it is causing damage to our spiritual structure. In a word, we need to strip our foundations and return to the bedrock: Jesus.

Third, *we will be held accountable for our choices and approach to life* (v. 13). It is true that as followers of Christ we will not be judged concerning our eternal destiny. That was settled at the cross, and when we placed our faith in Christ, our sins were forgiven and we received the gift of eternal life. But that doesn't mean we should live carelessly, following the whims of whatever we desire. According to this passage, we will be held accountable for what we do with our lives. The critical question is: What will be revealed when "the fire itself will test the quality of [your] work"?

This leads me to the fourth observation: *The enduring (eternal) quality of our lives will be rewarded* (vv. 12–14). Every day of our lives we must choose that which endures ("gold, silver, and precious stones") over that which may be so appealing but is perishable ("wood, hay, straw"). It is my view that this passage clearly teaches that although we are saved for eternity, some of us will experience the loss of reward because we settled for the perishable. In this regard, we're wasting our eternal wealth.

The burden of my heart, and the reason I'm writing this book, is that God has called us to be a people of destiny. We have a longing in our souls because eternity has been written in our hearts (Ecclesiastes 3:11). Eternity is a powerful motivation. Someone once said that if you have a *why* for living, you can stand almost any *how*. Our home in heaven is our motivation and destiny. When we live up to that sense of destiny at the center of our lives, we will experience purpose, passion, and perspective. We have been called to live for a time we cannot see.

It is my prayer that God will deeply touch your heart as you journey through these pages with me. I am praying that the reality of our heavenly destiny will produce in us compelling spiritual vibrancy and relevance that will draw others to follow the Savior who knows us and loves us.

Crawford W. Loritts Jr.

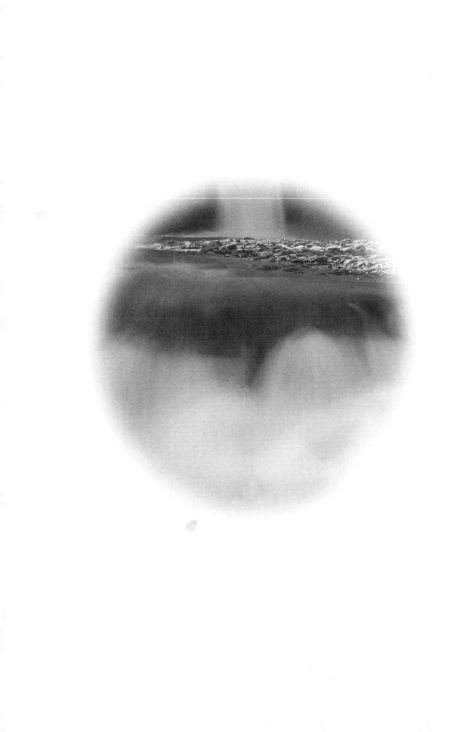

Live in the Light of the Cross

Do you find it hard to envision heaven? If so, you're not alone. And I suspect that's one reason why so many of us don't understand what it means to "live with an eternal perspective." We're not there yet! And we don't—can't—see as God sees. So we put heaven out of our minds, thinking, *I'll deal with that when the time comes. It's a long way off.*

Maybe. Maybe not.

But I believe God gives us a glimpse of eternal life by first letting us experience a new life here on earth. That was the experience of Harold Thompson.

Harold was a notorious bank robber who stole, literally, millions of dollars. He was finally caught, charged, convicted of armed robbery, and sentenced to life in prison. He was a pretty tough character and became one of the prison bosses. Many thought his sentence was permanent—not only a life of physical incarceration, but also a lifetime of sin and spiritual darkness.

But something happened to Harold. He heard the gospel

and eventually gave his life to Christ. He dramatically changed. He developed a hunger for the Word of God and a deep desire to see his fellow inmates come to Christ. Although he was behind bars, God set his soul free. And he took every opportunity to share that message with others.

Many of his fellow prisoners came to Christ, and Harold began a Bible study to help them grow in their faith. He became a model prisoner. Eventually, through an amazing chain of events, the president of the United States heard about his story and decided to pardon him. And when Harold Thompson was released, he became a part of the prison ministry of Campus Crusade for Christ.

In talking with Harold, it is readily apparent that he is a man who lives with profound gratitude that God stepped in to give him a second chance. He lives his new life committed to eternal priorities. And though our own stories may not appear to be as dramatic, God stepped into each of our lives to give us this same gift. We have been given new life, and we are going to be with Him forever.

The fact that you will live forever brings a sense of humble confidence about what you do right now.

The gift of eternal life also affects our time on earth because we no longer need to fear death. Think of it: If you are a believer—if you have given your life to Christ—death is not final. It is just a transition from one life to another, almost like walking through a door. Though death is sorrowful, it is not the end.

If you are not afraid of death, it releases you to live the Christian life with a sense of holy freedom. The fact that you will live forever brings a sense of humble confidence about what you do *right now.* You do not need to walk through life burdened by the worries and fears of this life.

IN JUST A MOMENT . . .

For you, as for me, it all began with a defining moment—a moment on which all history hangs.

You've probably heard the term *defining moment.* For example, September 11, 2001, stands as a defining moment in American history. The planes that were hijacked by terrorists and flown into the Twin Towers, the Pentagon, and crashed in western Pennsylvania forever changed the way we view our safety and security as Americans. I remember thinking that day that this was the first time in my lifetime that America had been attacked on her own soil. I sensed that things would never be the same in this country—and every time I go through security at an airport now, I am reminded how our way of life was altered on that sunny September morning.

When Karen and I were married on May 22, 1971—that was a defining moment. Even as we exchanged vows, I thought, *You're really going to have to step up here . . . you're the head of a household now.* In fact, as we stood in the receiving line during the reception, my father said to me, "Son, I want you to remember that Karen didn't ask to marry you—you asked to marry her. You better take care of her." I realized, whatever I was before this day, I ain't no longer!

And I remember standing in a hall at Riddell Memorial Hospital, looking into the newborn nursery and seeing our first child. As I gazed at that baby boy, my eyes filled with tears as I prayed, "God, help me to be the best dad that I possibly can be." I knew I had the charge and care not only of his physical well-being but also of his soul. That was a benchmark.

Often defining moments are dictated by circumstances outside of our control. The death of a loved one . . . an accident or illness or sudden calamity . . . or even an unexpected opportunity at work or in ministry—all of these situations force us to make decisions. What we do in response to these life invasions will determine the course of our lives.

Two thousand years ago, God orchestrated a defining moment so profound that the world still debates its meaning today. Through this one incredible act, He demands a response from every person born into this world. There's no such thing as choosing not to choose. To not respond favorably is to choose both a way of life apart from God and an ultimate destiny forever separated from Him. Our lives and our futures depend on our response to God's defining moment.

I'm speaking of the focal point of history—the death of Christ on the cross.

"What Do You Want from God?"

It was a Sunday morning in January 1964, and I was almost fourteen. Our pastor had finished preaching, and he asked those who sensed that they had a particular spiritual need to come and kneel at the altar.

In my heart I knew this was my moment. For several weeks I had been haunted by the question, *What will happen to me if I die? Where will I go?* Furthermore, I felt guilty because of the wrong things I had done. No one had to convince me that I was a sinner—I knew in my heart that I was guilty. God had made me aware of my need.

So that Sunday morning in 1964 was a divine appointment. Through our pastor's invitation, the Holy Spirit was forcing the issue in my heart. I was brought face-to-face with God's defining moment—the death of His Son on the cross. I knew I had to make a decision and settle the issue, and so I came to the altar.

My pastor knelt beside me and put his arm around my shoulder, asking, "Son, what is it you want from God?" I began to weep as I expressed my need to be forgiven and have Christ in my life. He led me in a prayer of repentance and faith. It was my defining moment. That day my life and destiny changed. My sins were forgiven, and I became a citizen of heaven.

To be sure, in the words of my dear friend Josh McDowell, there are many ways to Christ but only one way to God, and that is through Christ (John 14:6). We each have our own story about our spiritual journey—but at some point all of us must come to the cross. That is the place where lives are transformed and our future is determined.

I am concerned that too often we lose sight of the cross in how we do Christianity these days. We participate in church worship and ministry activities, and we spend time reading the Bible and growing in our relationship with God. We look for ways to feed the poor and heal broken marriages and keep our children unstained by the world and resist temptation and address cultural issues from a biblical perspective—and somehow the cross becomes a peripheral issue in our lives.

But the cross *is* Christianity. We live within its shadow, as D. L. Moody understood. When asked about the source of his success as a Christian and an evangelist, he would often say "Before I came to Christ, I worked toward the cross. After I came to Christ, I worked from the cross. The source and the secret is the cross."

HIS PASSION, OUR PENALTY

Mel Gibson's film *The Passion of the Christ* reminded us forcefully of why the cross matters. The months before and after the release of the movie saw a remarkable national debate unfolding. I found it amazing that questions like "Who killed Christ?" and "Why did Christ die on the cross?" were actually discussed on prime time, national television.

Many people assailed Gibson for his unsparing, gut-wrenching portrayal of Christ's suffering, for focusing so much on this one part of Jesus' time on earth, and even for relying too much on the gospel accounts. They feared the film would spark a wave of anti-Semitism. What these critics did not understand was the "why" behind the Passion—that Christ suffered and died to pay the penalty for our sins.

But many Christians did get it. They—we?—wept as they watched because they knew Christ endured each lash on the back, each agonizing step on the Via Dolorosa, each painful breath while hanging on the cross, because of the ugliness and enormity of their own sin. They thought of the selfishness and deceit and pettiness and cruelty that they fought on a daily basis, and marveled anew that their sins are forgiven because of what Christ went through for them/us on the cross.

You see, the focal point of Christ's mission in this world was to once and for all deal with the problem of sin. It was God's plan for His only Son to experience unimaginable suffering, to be tortured and hung on the cross for the sins of the world. What He went through for us is beyond human description. And to think that the God-man, Christ Jesus, as an act of His will, submitted to His Father's plan. As Jesus said in John 10:14–18:

"I am the good shepherd; and I know My own and My own know Me, even as the Father knows Me and I know the Father; and I lay down My life for the sheep. And I have other sheep, which are not of this fold; I must bring them also, and they shall hear My voice; and they shall become one flock with one shepherd. For this reason the Father loves Me, because I lay down My life that I may take it again. No one has taken it away from Me, but I lay it down on My own initiative. I have authority to lay it down, and I have authority to take it up again. This commandment I received from My Father."

In his description of the willing submission of the Savior to suffer on our behalf, the apostle Paul says in Philippians 2:8, "And being found in appearance as a man, He humbled Himself by becoming obedient to the point of death, even death on a cross." That last phrase, "even death on a cross," underlines an incredible irony—that innocent royalty was submitted to a common criminal's death.

The cross was a means of capital punishment throughout the Roman Empire, reserved for the worst murderers and other despised criminals. The cross was created to punish the guilty —and that's the point. Jesus was *not* guilty. He was sinless, but He bore our guilt and our sin.

As Jesus hung on the cross, He uttered three words just before he died: "It is finished" (John 19:30). He was not referring to the end of His physical suffering on the cross. He was talking about the completion of His mission, the fulfillment of God's plan. The debt was paid in full. Nothing else needs to be done.

Pastor C. J. Mahaney said it well: "The Christian who desires to live a cross-centered life will regularly face his or her own depravity and the seriousness of personal sin, squarely and unflinchingly. It's a reality. But the reality of the death and resurrection of Jesus for the forgiveness of sin is even greater."[1]

I don't know about you, but this truth—this profound, severe grace and mercy—causes me to bow in worship and adoration to our awesome God. His love for us is both incomprehensible and unspeakable.

WE BECOME SLAVES OF WHATEVER WE YIELD OURSELVES TO.

I am reminded of a man I know who accumulated an incredible credit card debt. He had grown accustomed to a rather extravagant lifestyle and had an addiction to things. He was using credit cards to pay other credit card bills. Finally, his "smoke and mirrors" game caught up with him. He could no longer manipulate the system. The chickens came home to roost, and he had to declare bankruptcy.

Similarly, we were born morally and spiritually bankrupt. But the good news is that when we acknowledge and declare our spiritual bankruptcy before God, He forgives us and pours upon us the riches of His grace (Ephesians 1:3–8).

EVERYDAY SURRENDER

But that's not all!

When we commit our lives to Christ, we not only receive forgiveness of sin but we are also given the gift of eternal life. Our future is changed—as Harold Thompson found out. By placing our faith in Christ, we are no longer condemned to eternal separation. We are given a new life, an eternal life; we know we will live with Him forever in a special place reserved for us (John 14:1–3). By giving us this gift, God is in effect declaring, "My child, I love you so much that I want you with Me forever." It says that He has bought us, purchased us, and we are His (1 Peter 1:18–20 and Ephesians 1:13–14).

But how does this affect the way we live our lives day in,

day out? When we placed our faith in Jesus Christ, then the crucified, resurrected Son of God came to take up residence in our lives. In some mysterious and profound way, we by faith have experienced His crucifixion ("I have been crucified with Christ," Galatians 2:20). Sin's controlling power over our lives has been broken. Sin is always with us; never are we going to be sinless and perfect in this life. However, we do have a perfect Savior living inside us.

We become slaves of whatever we yield ourselves to (Romans 6). And because Jesus has broken the power of sin over us, we have to choose, on a moment-by-moment basis, to yield to the victorious Christ who lives within us. When we yield to the indwelling Christ, He lives His life in and through us and empowers us to overcome sin. In this regard, victory over sin or conquering sin is the result of moment-by-moment surrender to the power of the cross.

This power also allows us to declare and maintain our allegiance to the One who has changed our lives. When empowered by the Spirit, we are not ashamed of the cross. To be a follower of Christ means to be a member of the community of the cross. Jesus said in Matthew 10:38, "And he who does not take his cross and follow after Me is not worthy of Me." In other words, we should be willing to identify with all that the cross means and implies—not just forgiveness and eternal life, but also times of suffering and rejection. We say yes to all that the cross calls for.

Paul put it this way in Galatians 6:14: "May it never be that I should boast, except in the cross of our Lord Jesus Christ, through which the world has been crucified to me, and I to the world." This does not imply we should not enjoy this life and some of the good pleasures this world has to offer—but when we surrender our lives to Christ, He claims all of us: every thought, every action, every moment.

"IN REMEMBRANCE OF ME"

We must never forget the cross; it should be like the wallpaper on our computer screen. We should live our lives against the backdrop of the cross.

This is why every follower of Christ should regularly celebrate communion, as Paul declares in I Corinthians 11:23–26:

For I received from the Lord that which I also delivered to you, that the Lord Jesus in the night in which He was betrayed took bread; and when He had given thanks, He broke it and said, "This is My body, which is for you; do this in remembrance of Me." In the same way He took the cup also, after supper, saying, "This cup is the new covenant in My blood; do this, as often as you drink it, in remembrance of Me." For as often as you eat this bread and drink the cup, you proclaim the Lord's death until He comes.

Communion is a call to remember the suffering of our Savior on our behalf—to not forget what He has done, what He has given to us, and who we are. One of my most tender, cherished childhood memories has to do with a communion service. At the church where our family attended, we celebrated communion on the first Sunday of every month. As a young boy of perhaps five or six, I sat on the pew between my mother and father. As they passed the elements, the congregation would sing, "Let Us Break Bread Together." And even as I write these words, I can still hear those sweet sounds of the congregation singing:

Let us break bread together on our knees.
Let us break bread together on our knees.
When I fall on my knees with my face to the rising sun,
Oh Lord, have mercy on me.

Let us drink wine together on our knees.
Let us drink wine together on our knees.
When I fall on my knees with my face to the rising sun,
Oh Lord, have mercy on me.

Let us praise God together on our knees.
Let us praise God together on our knees.
When I fall on my knees with my face to the rising sun,
Oh Lord, have mercy on me.

I remember one particular day when I looked up at my mother as she sang along, and I watched tears of remembrance fill her eyes and slowly run down her cheeks. She loved Jesus, and she had experienced the power of the cross. She was living in the light of that single defining moment that changed history.

Are you living in that light?

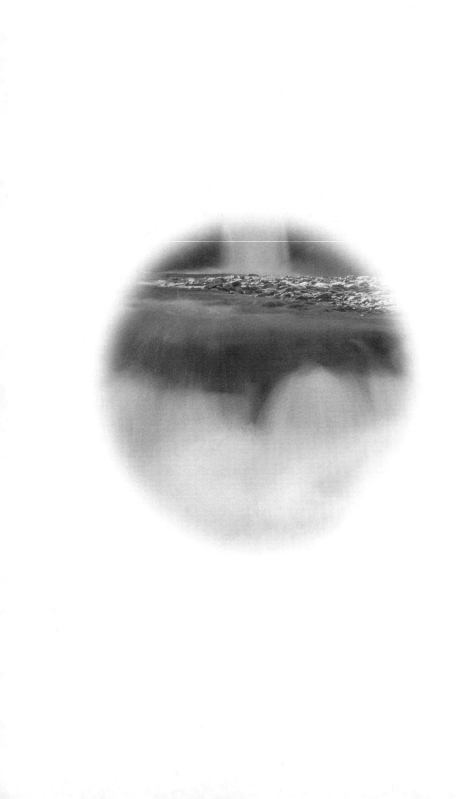

Keep Your Eyes on the Prize

Every now and then, the curtain between this life on earth and life forever with God parts slightly—and we are able to get a glimpse of what we have in store.

My older sister, Elaina, was fifty-six years old and suffering from breast cancer. Near the end of her life, she slipped into a coma. The doctors said it was just a matter of time. But something strange happened.

On a Sunday afternoon, while her best friend, Barbara, was sitting next to her bed, Elaina regained consciousness and began speaking. Karen and I were in the car returning from church when my cell phone rang. Barbara said, "You're not going to believe this. Elaina is awake and talking." She held the phone next to Elaina, and for what would be the final time in this world, I heard her voice: "C. W.," she said, using my family nickname, "He is a mighty God. He's a mighty God. And I'm going to see Him."

As tears rolled down my cheeks I said, "That's right, Elaina, you're going to see Him soon."

That evening, at 7:20 p.m., she passed into His presence. She joined my parents, who passed away a few years earlier, and they are now rejoicing around the throne.

This is where the Word becomes real—*lived*. This is where those eloquent resurrection passages from Paul in I Corinthians 15 take on an immediate and vibrant significance. As I wept at the loss of my beloved sister, at the same time the Lord brought to mind the triumphant affirmation that death did *not* destroy Elaina, nor Mom or Pop. It is worth quoting in full the apostle's wondrous description of our final destiny.

Let these words grab your heart and capture your imagination:

> *Now I say this, brethren, that flesh and blood cannot inherit the kingdom of God; nor does the perishable inherit the imperishable. Behold, I tell you a mystery; we will not all sleep, but we shall all be changed, in a moment, in the twinkling of an eye, at the last trumpet; for the trumpet will sound, and the dead will be raised imperishable, and we shall be changed. For this perishable must put on the imperishable, and this mortal must put on immortality. But when this perishable will have put on the imperishable, and this mortal will have put on immortality, then will come about the saying that is written, "Death is swallowed up in victory. O death, where is your victory? O death, where is your sting?" The sting of death is sin, and the power of sin is the law; but thanks be to God, who gives us the victory through our Lord Jesus Christ. Therefore, my beloved brethren, be steadfast, immovable, always abounding in the work of the Lord, knowing that your toil is not in vain in the Lord.*
>
> —I Corinthians 15:50–58

These—and other promises of eternity—are, as Peter puts it, a "living hope," not just dry words on a page. The resurrection of Christ has conquered death for the believer. Any Christian who dies is immediately ushered into the presence of the Lord (2 Corinthians 5:1–8). And all who have died in Him will be raised in the future.

This truth, this realization, this *destiny* brings into focus what we do in this life. Because we know where we are going, we have a sense of what we are to do *now.* Listen again to Paul: "Therefore, my beloved brethren, be steadfast, immovable, always abounding in the work of the Lord, knowing that your toil is not in vain in the Lord."

But we have to have a plan.

"REMEMBER YOU ARE GOING SOMEWHERE"

I'm a firm believer in goal setting. When our children were growing up, Karen and I would take a family vacation every year just before the kids went back to school. We made some great memories with trips to places like Hilton Head, South Carolina, and Gatlinburg, Tennessee.

*H*OW DOES THIS ACTIVITY CONTRIBUTE TO WHAT YOU SAID YOU WANT TO ACCOMPLISH OR WHO YOU WANT TO BECOME?

But before we returned home each year, each child also had to complete an assignment —a list of goals for the upcoming school year. They wrote down what they wanted to accomplish in their spiritual lives, in academics, in their character, and in other areas of their lives. For example, our son Bryndan, a very energetic little guy, sometimes had trouble controlling all his energy when he was in elementary school. (He was his father's child in that respect; I had the same problem when I was young!) So one of his goals was "Obey my teachers." As the children grew, goals would change—another son, Bryan, wanted to make his high school football team.

We would challenge the children to establish spiritual goals such as reading the Bible on a daily basis. Throughout the year, Karen and I would pray that God would enable each child to accomplish these goals. Then we would regularly check with them on their progress. The process helped them to make choices about where they were going with their lives. For example, whenever a particular child's behavior did not square with his or her goals, we would ask, "How does this activity contribute to what you said you want to accomplish or who you want to become?"

This forced some difficult decisions on their part. If a child wasn't reading the Bible regularly, we would ask, "Didn't you say you were going to do that on a daily basis? Is it a priority? Well, what are you going to do to make sure that happens?"

Karen and I wanted our children to see the benefits of setting goals. Goals have a way of bringing order and direction to your life. They keep you moving. They give you something to work toward. Goals help you to live life intentionally and focus on what is most important. On more than one occasion I would say to a child, "Remember you are going somewhere, and not all roads will get you there. Don't be distracted. Keep your eyes on where you are going."

Lives That Tell the Truth

It occurs to me that I could pass on the same advice to many Christians today. I think too many of us are passively living the Christian life. We don't intend to do so, but we're so busy simply living day to day that we lose sight of what's important. Our physical and spiritual reserves are depleted because we don't get the rest we need, and we don't spend quality time with the Lord. So we live reactively rather than proactively, bumping along from one crisis to the next. We snap at our families and are burdened by fear and anxiety.

Now, to be sure, God is in control of the events and circumstances of our lives, and He will allow plenty of "surprises" along the way to our ultimate destination. But that's the point—no matter what happens in this life, we must never lose sight of our destination. We need to keep our eyes on where we are going, because where we are going shapes how we live now. Do our lives tell the truth about where we are going? How does our behavior, our approach to life, square with where we are ultimately headed?

When followers of Christ live with the motivation of heaven at the core of their beings, it puts flesh around evangelism. People are not only drawn to the message that we share but also to the credibility of the lives that we lead.

Look again at the I Corinthians 15 text. When Paul speaks of "knowing that your toil is not in vain in the Lord," it is a motivational summary statement of chapter 15. It is as if Paul is saying, "I've reminded you of where you are going. You don't need to worry about what will happen when you die—you will be with God forever. So go out and pour yourself into serving Him without reservation."

Simply put, we are called to adopt an attitude of complete and intentional service to Jesus Christ. Not all of us are called to full-time professional ministry, but as Christians we serve Him full-time. All we do is directed by Him and is an act of service to Him, whether we are musicians, managers, car salesmen, or computer technicians. Whatever you do is to be viewed as a calling from God and a vehicle to serve the Lord Jesus Christ.

And because we don't know when we are going to die or

when He is going to return, there should be a seriousness and urgency about our service. Let's consider three aspects of this attitude of complete, intentional service that we can see in I Corinthians 15:58.

1. THIS ONE THING I DO: STAYING FOCUSED

In light of our imminent translation into His presence, we are told to be "steadfast." This is the idea of staying focused, not being distracted. It implies that we know what God has placed before us to do, and we give ourselves completely to getting it done.

On several occasions I have had the opportunity to speak to professional football teams during Super Bowl week. The environment surrounding the Super Bowl is always one of absolute madness; thousands of fans pour into the host city and most of them quickly find the hotels where the players are staying. It's a mob scene—the hotel lobbies are jammed with fans clamoring for autographs, and the media is everywhere with cameras and microphones. The athletes, coaches, and in recent years their families, are interviewed about everything from what they ate for breakfast to their favorite colors. Distractions are everywhere, and it's easy for the players to forget that they are actually there to play a football game.

For that reason, two days before Super Bowl Sunday the teams will move to an undisclosed location, often miles outside of the city. Coaches know they need to get rid of distractions so players can recapture their focus. It's hard to be successful if your mind is not settled and locked into the task at hand.

Do you know what you are supposed to do with your life?

What is it that God has placed in your heart to do? Are you diligently pursuing that calling by giving it your undivided, undistracted attention? Over the years I have encountered many Christians who know what God has called them to do, but for whatever reason, they are not able to shake free from distractions. So many are not as effective as they could be because they are not willing to say, *"This one thing I do."*

I can think of a company whose focused efforts have made them a great success. This outstanding restaurant chain is Chick-fil-A. Some years ago I was invited to speak at their annual corporate seminar, where they bring together their company leaders and the operators of their restaurants. During the conference I had the privilege of sharing a meal with Truett Cathy, the legendary founder and chairman of Chick-fil-A. I asked him, "How do you account for your incredible success as a company?"

In his humble, gracious way he said, "We came along at a time when no one was doing exactly what we're doing." He went on to say, "At Chick-fil-A we stick to what we do best, and that's a hearty breast of chicken." And with a twinkle in his eye, he remarked, "You know, Crawford, success in life is knowing what your chicken sandwich is!"

That conversation caused me to take a long, hard look at my own commitments. My time and energy were getting eaten up by various administrative tasks that someone else should have been doing. I needed to give my attention to my own "chicken sandwich"—the speaking and writing God has given me to do. These things reflect the primary gifting that God has given me.

Truett Cathy's words reminded me of something that I had known but ignored—that just because you can do something doesn't necessarily mean that you *ought* to do it. Distractions are sneaky and subtle. God's assignments for us demand a vigilant focus if we are going to be effective.

Let me ask you: When is the last time you took a look at how you are really using your time and your energy? God gives us a task to perform in the context of uncertainty. We don't know when our time is up. We need to be prepared to offer to Him the gift of a faithful, diligent heart.

2. Immovable Objects: The Power of Perseverance

In I Corinthians 15:58, Paul says we are to be "immovable." In the original Greek language, this word is *ametakenasis*, which literally means "not with motion." Whereas diligence ("steadfastness") has to do with identifying what is most important and not moving away from your focus, being "immovable" means perseverance—not quitting because of pressure or adversity.

Because our eternal future is more secure than wherever we may be in this life, we should embrace what God has called us to do with that same eternal sense of security. We persevere because the work to which God assigns us touches time with eternity—and whenever we quit we in essence declare that this life and this world's values are more important than God's direction for our lives.

There is something to that old line, "The true measure of a person's greatness is not seen in what they accomplish, but in what it takes to stop them." I am reminded of the story of John and Vera May Perkins, who were born and raised in rural Mississippi during the dark days of Jim Crow and segregation. When they moved to Southern California to escape the pain and oppression of racial injustice, John vowed he would never return to Mississippi.

Life was good for John and Vera May in California. But John sensed something was missing in his life. One day his young son told him that he had attended a neighborhood Bible club and had asked Jesus into his heart. John knew instinctively that *this* was what he was missing, and so it wasn't long before John also surrendered his life to Jesus Christ. He was so grateful for the gift of eternal life that he placed his entire life in God's hands.

A strange desire began to grip John's heart. He sensed God was calling their family to return to the place he had vowed he would never go back to—not only to reach his family and friends for Christ, but also to instill hope, dignity, and build communities of love and justice among his people.

*M*ORE OFTEN THAN NOT, GOD CALLS US TO SOMETHING NOT AWAY FROM SOMETHING.

When John began his ministry, he was met with fierce opposition by racist white people in positions of power. They tried to intimidate him and drive him out of Mississippi. Police beat him nearly to death. But he knew that along his journey toward heaven, God had given him this assignment, so he wouldn't quit. But not only did he refuse to leave, he also refused to hate anyone—even those who beat him.

Today, God has allowed John and Vera May Perkins to live to see some of the enormous fruit of their perseverance and faithfulness. John Perkins is a living legend and is known as the father of modern urban ministry. His books and articles have impacted literally millions, not to mention the impact of his involvement in conferences, organizations, and churches that he helped establish. There are many, many people who will be in heaven because the Perkinses did not shrink back from completing God's assignments for their lives. Many of us are committed to authentic racial reconciliation because of the example and price that they paid.

Only the values of eternity would cause anyone to endure what they did. That's being heavenly minded. But during those dark days, the Perkinses had no idea that God was going to produce a bumper crop through their suffering, or how He was using them at the time. They just did what God called them to do.

You may be wondering when it *is* okay to quit. During over thirty years of ministry, Karen and I have served with three organizations. We left the first two when we sensed that God was finished with our service there. He made this clear to us, and we moved on to His next assignment for us. But we didn't leave either of the ministries because of difficulties and hard times.

Generally speaking, it is not a good idea to quit just because you are going through hard times. More often than not, God calls us *to* something not away from something. God uses what He calls us to to make us what He wants us to be. In the words of the famous American preacher Phillips Brooks, "Do not pray for tasks equal to your powers. Pray for power equal to your tasks." The doing of the work is not the miracle; no, we *become* the miracle in the process of doing the work.

I know a man who has bounced around from one ministry to the next. In fact, for a number of years he worked with our organization, Campus Crusade for Christ, and transferred to several different ministries within our organization. He is a very gifted man with a lot of dreams. But whenever he would experience some adversity and "feel the heat," he would suddenly announce that God had called him to move on. Yet I always sensed that God really hadn't been involved in his decision. One day I told him, "God won't give you what you want because you won't stick around long enough to get what you need." It's a shame, because he remains a man with unfulfilled potential and unrealized dreams.

An important distinction needs to be kept in mind. To serve Christ is not the same as selecting "a career path." God has given us gifts, talents, and opportunities—but not for us to arbitrarily choose what *we* would like to do and what would make *us* most fulfilled. He gives us these things so that He can use them. We seek to understand His will and His assignments for our lives—through the study of His Word, prayer, the leading of the Holy Spirit, and the advice of others. And then once this is clear, we pour our lives into what He has assigned us to do, and we do not move away from that path until He moves us.

This gives definition to perseverance. Perseverance, although difficult at times, is the grateful price we pay to implement God's assignments for our lives. Perseverance is the noble response to the God of the universe who gives us the privilege and honor to serve Him.

3. SERVE THE LORD WITH EXCELLENCE

Looking again at 1 Corinthians 15:58, Paul says we should be "always abounding in the work of the Lord." The term *abounding* conveys the idea of both urgency and quality: getting the job done because we are up against the clock, but also concentrating on quality because what we do will be examined.

When I was growing up, Saturday mornings were reserved for cleaning up the house. My sisters and I had specific chores that our parents expected us to do. Sometimes they would leave to run some errands, and always as they walked out the door they would call out, "When we return, we expect your work to be done."

We knew what they meant. We needed to get in gear, get the work done, and get it right. Mom was a bit of a perfectionist, and there would be consequences if our work wasn't finished or if it was shoddy.

As Christians we are on our way to meeting the King. And, as we saw earlier, He will examine our work; we will be held accountable for what we have done. The question is: What are we doing with what God has given us? Are we giving our best in getting it done?

Our journey here on earth is brief. All we have is this moment in history. And because we know where we are going, this moment must be completely used for the honor and glory of God. So we gladly approach whatever He has given us to do with whatever tools He has given us—with intention, focus, and a spirit of excellence.

Because we—like my sister Elaina, like John Perkins—know where we are going, we serve now with obedience and with faithfulness. These things are the earthly "coal" that will produce eternal diamonds—a treasure that will be passed on both now and to future generations.

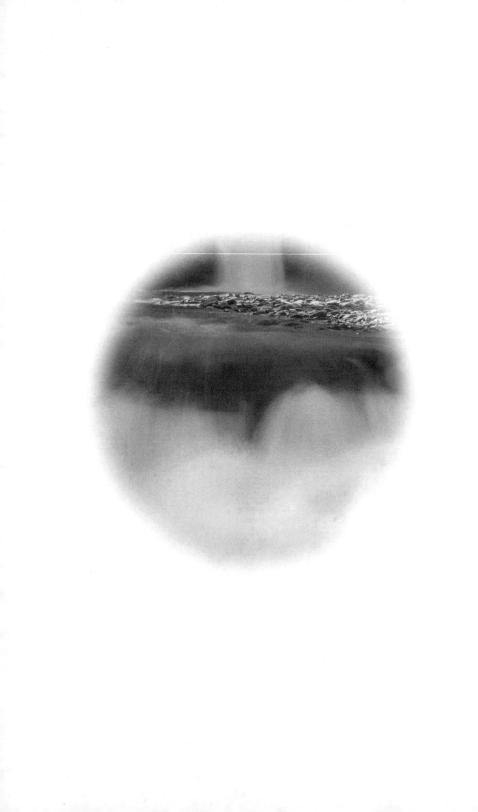

Letting
God Lead
Your Life

Sometimes it seems as if half of America wants to be famous.

Look at the popularity of the so-called reality shows like *The Apprentice, Wife Swap* (where real-life wives trade places to live with each other's families for a time), *Survivor,* and the various home-makeover series. We love seeing a former no-body attain instant fame, however briefly. Young people in particular love celebrities and imagine what it would be like to be in the spotlight.

But even those of us past celebrity-worship age love the idea of being important. We pursue accomplishment, achievement, reputation—significance. We admire those who've gone to the "right" colleges, who've "made something" of themselves. We encourage our kids to do the same. We want to be friends of the important. And we enjoy showing off the fruits of our achievements—often, the sleek new cars, trendy attire, and electronic toys advertised on reality shows and popular television! And each step along the way, as we collect friends and possessions and accomplishments, we ask ourselves, "Are we significant yet?"

Holy Tension

Right now you're probably expecting me to say, "Friend, God doesn't care about your significance." The truth is, He does—but not in the way we tend to think.

Let me be clear. We are significant in God's sight, and God created us to live significant lives. I believe the inner desire we have to "make a statement" with our lives is part of the image of God stamped all over our being. But the statement is to be focused on God, not on man. We live for Him and, with the profound sense of our destiny, for heaven.

God makes His statement through our lives.

This can create a bit of a holy tension as we live the Christian life. Within us lies a longing to be with Jesus; but at the same time, we also desire to do all that we can for Him during our time on earth. Paul understood the problem:

What then? Only that in every way, whether in pretense or in truth, Christ is proclaimed; and in this I rejoice, yes, and I will rejoice. For I know that this shall turn out for my deliverance through your prayers and the provision of the Spirit of Jesus Christ, according to my earnest expectation and hope, that I shall not be put to shame in anything, but that with all boldness, Christ shall even now, as always, be exalted in my body, whether by life or by death. For to me, to live is Christ, and to die is gain. But if I am to live on in the flesh, this will mean fruitful labor for me; and I do not know which to choose. But I am hard-pressed from both directions, having the desire to depart and be with Christ, for that is very much better; yet to remain on in the flesh is more necessary for your sake. —Philippians 1:18–24

Remember, Paul was writing this in a cold, dank, poorly lit prison, possibly chained to his Roman guard around-the-clock. I imagine the prospect of "depart[ing] and be[ing] with Christ" seemed very inviting to him. But he had made a choice that gave eternal significance to his life—that "with all boldness, Christ shall even now, as always, be exalted in my body, whether by life or by death. For to me, to live is Christ, and to die is gain" (vv. 20–21).

When we truly realize we are here on this earth for an all-too-brief moment, and like Paul we choose to live this life for the honor and glory of God, we enjoy an absolutely "no lose" proposition. The game is fixed, the outcome is guaranteed. God makes His statement through our lives.

That, my friend, is significance beyond human description. But if we do *not* live in light of this decision—if we invest ourselves in empty pursuits—we will someday be looking out the window of our big, empty house, wondering what it all added up to.

AFTER THE FIRE

I'm not saying it's wrong to desire achievement or a comfortable lifestyle. I am saying, however, that these things need to be kept in perspective—as a pastor friend of mine learned. You see, his house burned to the ground one Sunday morning while he and his wife were in church. In fact, he says the house was on fire while he was preaching. All they had left was what they took to church with them that morning. Everything else—furniture, appliances, clothes, books, personal items—literally went up in smoke.

My friend told me that what he and his wife miss most are the things that the insurance check cannot replace: photo albums, letters and notes, gifts that don't have much monetary value but are priceless nonetheless. I know what he means. I sit as I write in a room surrounded by treasures. On the wall in front of me is a marriage covenant Karen and I signed. All around are framed pictures of our children and our three grandsons. Each picture has its own story—warm, tender memories, some representing significant milestones in our kids' lives.

On another wall in a lovely frame is our family tree, written in my grandfather's hand. Next to me is my prayer journal, the most recent addition of many that I have here at the house. These journals chart my walk and relationship with the Lord. If our house went up in smoke, these are some of the things Karen and I would miss the most. All of the other things—furniture, appliances, even the house itself—are not nearly as important.

When we invest ourselves in people—when we have a passion for God and want to share that passion with others, then we're living with an eye toward heaven!

"A Brief Adventure"

Few people understood this better than Bill Bright. As a young man, Bill dreamed of wealth and achievement. He moved from Oklahoma to Los Angeles in the mid-1940s and began building a successful business. But it was also apparent that God had designs upon the life of Bill Bright. The very first day he arrived in Southern California, he met a group of dynamic Christians, and eventually he became a believer himself through the ministry of Hollywood Presbyterian Church. Over the next few years, his life changed drastically, and he began spending more and more of his time helping people come to know the Savior.

Soon after he was married, he and his wife, Vonette, decided to write a contract with God, acknowledging that He owned everything that He placed in their hands. "When I had first proposed to Vonette," Bill writes, "we had once talked about a honeymoon in Europe, about securing the finest voice teacher to develop her already beautiful singing voice, and about living in the fabulous Bel-Air district of Los Angeles. But now all that had been given to Christ. Such ambitions had become secondary, if not nonexistent."[2]

They went on to live their lives as joyful, surrendered servants, slaves of Jesus Christ. In 1951 they began Campus Crusade for Christ, which became one of the largest and most influential evangelical ministries in the world.

Shortly before Bill Bright died in 2003, he wrote a book entitled *The Journey Home*. Early on in the book he described the inner motivation that always drove him during his journey on earth:

> During the last fifty years I have traveled many millions of miles ministering to our staff and their disciples, students, and laymen in most countries of the world. Through the years I have experienced the truth that God is real. His promises are true. Time on earth is an exciting, but brief adventure, and heaven is my home. Without question it is a joyous journey.
>
> There is a longing in every human heart for some place to call home. According to their circumstances, people may try to make their dwelling places on earth as heavenly as possible. Safe, bright, arrayed with vistas, full of love and peace. For the followers of Jesus, heaven is the home where you come knowing Jesus Christ as Lord and Savior. The heavenly father God greets you and because of his faithfulness to his promises, you can be assured that you will be admitted.[3]

When I read those words, I said to myself, "Bill Bright has it right." Heaven—our home, our reward, our destiny—gives weight, meaning, and significance to our lives here on earth. When we embrace this perspective, then we bring "eternal weight" to bear on this "exciting but brief adventure."

Friend, what about you? If we have placed Jesus Christ truly at the center of our lives, then as Lord He determines and directs what we do with our lives. Let me plead with you. Take a look at how you are really living and what actually is important to you. Be honest with yourself. Are you completely surrendered to Jesus Christ? Does your life reflect the values of heaven?

If not, let me encourage you to take your hands off your life. Place all of your dreams, desires, and expectations in His hands. Confess and repent of sin and self-centeredness. Determine in your heart that, like Paul, from now on Christ will be exalted in your body, "whether by life or by death."

ON THEIR SHOULDERS

Let's not underestimate the challenge we face. Because we do walk through a world that promotes values often opposed to those we find in the Bible, our resolve to live a life of heavenly significance will be tested. And sometimes we will give in to the pull of this world. When that happens, we need to quickly turn to our heavenly Father and once again confess our sin and renew our commitment.

Every morning when I wake up, the first thing I do is slip out of bed and come before the Lord in prayer. I seek Him and ask Him to guard my heart and my day. I realize how vulnerable I am and how susceptible I am to the temptation to buy into the culture's definition of significance. In a sense, this daily exercise is a fresh surrender of all that I am to Him and a constant reminder that my significance in this life is determined by Him and by my focus on heaven.

As part of this fresh, daily surrender, I often need to remind myself of a few perspectives on this heavenly significance. First is the realization that *you cannot fully determine the significance of your life.* Future generations and eternity will give the verdict concerning the depth and the complete picture of the contribution of our lives.

Hebrews 11:35–40 speaks of believers who, although they went through great hardships on earth, now see the promised Messiah face-to-face:

> *Women received back their dead by resurrection; and others were tortured, not accepting their release, in order that they might obtain a better resurrection; and others experienced mockings and scourgings, yes, also chains and imprisonment. They were stoned, they were sawn in two, they were tempted, they were put to death with the sword; they went about in sheepskins, in goatskins, being destitute, afflicted, ill-treated (men of whom the world was not worthy), wandering in deserts and mountains and caves and holes in the ground. And all these, having gained approval through their faith, did not receive what was promised, because God had provided something better for us, so that apart from us they should not be made perfect.*

This passage reminds me of my great-grandfather, Peter Loritts, whom I described in my book *Never Walk Away*. Peter was born into slavery in North Carolina. We know very little about the particulars of his life or his formative years. But we do know that he loved the Lord Jesus. Peter lived to a ripe old age, and my father remembered watching Peter sit on the front porch for hours, quietly singing hymns and praying. Although he couldn't read, he loved the Bible, and he would have his children and grandchildren read favorite passages to him.

Peter never traveled far from the old homestead there in
Catawba County, North Carolina. His remains are buried behind Thomas Chapel Methodist Church underneath an indis-
cernible headstone. If you think about it, in every way that we
measure significance and value in our world, Peter Loritts appeared to live a decidedly unremarkable life. He was just an il-
literate, uncelebrated former slave who happened to deeply
love God and be committed to his family.

Yet Peter passed this twin passion along to his son, Milton, who picked up the torch and placed it in my dad's hands.
My dad and mom modeled and poured this passion into their
children. They intentionally imprinted our lives with Jesus and
a heart for home. And every day of my life I think about my
dad, and I suppose several times in any given week my mind
drifts toward the stories about my grandfather and Peter. In a
very real sense, their lives and their passions are lived out
through me and now through my children.

On a recent Friday evening, I reluctantly pulled myself
away from a basketball playoff game on television to accompany
my wife to a formal banquet for an organization for which she
volunteers. When we walked into the meeting room, to my total surprise, I discovered that the evening was actually a cele-
bration held in my honor, commemorating the faithfulness of
God through my life and ministry. It was a humbling experience as different friends highlighted some of the things God
has done through me—the books I have written, the millions
of people I have spoken to through the years at various events,
the breadth and impact of our radio program, the boards I
serve on, leadership positions I have held. Our children were
there and gave moving tributes.

As I sat there overwhelmed and engulfed in the love, encouragement, and affirmation of hundreds of my friends and

family, my mind returned to Peter, Milton, and my parents. I thought of the sacrifices they had made, and how proud they would be if they could have experienced this evening. I began to choke back the tears.

And I was struck by the thought: "Could this be what Peter prayed about on the front porch?"

I receive more recognition than my parents and grandparents ever had. But recognition and greatness are two very different things. Greatness is buried behind Thomas Chapel, where Peter and Milton were laid, and side by side at Old Dominion cemetery in Roanoke, Virginia, at the graves of my parents. Their bodies were buried, but these great souls live on in the greatest place of all—and I will see them again. They hoisted me on their shoulders and believed God for what they could not experience in their own generation. They served in obscurity, but they lived faithfully.

This realization reminds me to never get full of myself. The blessings and impact of my life and ministry may not really be about me at all. I could simply be the focal point of the answered prayers of previous generations.

I think God probably chuckles and shakes His head at our little feeble attempts at measuring the significance of our lives. Faith is a continuum that cannot be fully determined, appreciated, or quantified when we try to wrap our arms around it in this life. Our true significance, our true legacy, is often seen in how we impact a time that we cannot see.

POSITIONS AND PLATFORMS

I am a visiting professor at Trinity Evangelical Divinity School in Deerfield, Illinois, outside of Chicago. In the spring I teach a course, "The Essence of Biblical Leadership." (It's an

entire semester compressed into one week!) In our culture today we tend to view dynamic leaders with great esteem. I've
heard parents speak of how they are teaching their children to
be leaders, not followers. But one of the anchor perspectives
of my course is this: *Nowhere in the Bible will you find leadership described primarily as a position. God gives the posi-
tion to lead as a platform to serve and to express His
heart and character to others.*

*I*T IS YOUR
HOLY AMBITION
TO BE CHRIST-
LIKE AND
NOT SIMPLY
SKILLED AND
PROFICIENT AT
DOING THE
WORK OF
CHRIST.

Paul understood our tendency to ele-
vate and emulate leaders. It was one of the
first issues he addressed in his first letter to
the quarrelsome Corinthians (1:10–17).
These followers were afflicted with a bad
case of hero worship, and Paul recognized
the harm such fixation on individuals was
inflicting on the cause of Christ. Basically
he told the church to tone it down and put
it in perspective. And in I Corinthians 4:1–2
he declares, "Let a man regard us in this
manner, as servants of Christ, and stewards
of the mysteries of God. In this case, more-
over, it is required of stewards that one be found trustworthy."

It's as if he's saying, "Okay, I see the pedestal you have
placed me on. I read the brochure and the publicity packet you
put together about me. Now give me the privilege of telling
you how I want you to view me and what I consider to be most
important about me."

Years ago when my ministry began, the Holy Spirit impressed on my heart that I was to never ask for a speaking en-
gagement or seek any position of leadership. Over the years this
conviction has developed into an approach, a philosophy of
ministry. I suppose it could be called "the servant's demeanor."

Let me share four brief points about servanthood:

- Don't ever tell God how to use you. You are His servant and your response is always yes, no matter what He tells you to do. Don't assume that His assignments will always line up with your gifts, talents, abilities, and background.
- What God has for you, no mortal being can take from you. Therefore serve Christ with a humble sense of holy confidence. You never need to compete or compare. Celebrate the joys, victories, and accomplishments of others.
- Don't live by your rights, but respond to what is right. People who live by their rights only reach the level of their demands. It is a painful truth, but there are times in which in order to become like Christ, our rights have to be violated.
- Don't live by your gifts, talents, and abilities, but cherish brokenness and surrender. It is your holy ambition to be Christlike and not simply skilled and proficient at doing the work of Christ.

In I Corinthians 4:1–2 we find one more phrase that Paul uses to describe himself. He says he wants to be known as a steward *"of the mysteries of God."* Paul's life and ministry belong to God. He is simply the manager of what belongs to him, and so are we. In verse 2, Paul mentions the primary responsibility of every steward: "It is required of stewards that one be found trustworthy." Because we are His servants, God gives us assignments. He has given us the gift of eternal life and set before us gifts, talents, responsibilities, and opportunities. He is holding us responsible for the faithful use of these things in accomplishing His will and mission for our lives.

That is the point of the story of the "talents" in Matthew

25:14–30. There is a man who goes on a long trip and entrusts his resources to three of his servants. He gives them "talents" (in those days, a talent was worth about a thousand dollars in silver content and probably much more in buying content). But he doesn't give them equal amounts. One servant receives five talents, another two talents, and the third is given just one. But all three are expected to use what had been given to them.

The first two invest the money wisely, while the last servant takes his talent and buries it in the ground. When the master returns and asks for an accounting, the two servants who made money on their investments are rewarded and honored. But our last servant offers a lame excuse: "I was afraid, and went away and hid your talent in the ground; see, you have what is yours." He is rebuked by his master.

If we have trusted Christ, our eternal destiny is secure in Him. We will be with Him in heaven. But that doesn't mean we are free to approach God's assignments for our lives any way we want to. With a calling comes an expectation. There will be a day of reckoning in which the Lord will ask us, "How did you use what I gave you?" Our accountability should motivate us to do the best we can with what we have.

One of my favorite songs is the contemporary classic "Find Us Faithful." Songwriter Steve Green took his inspiration from Hebrews 11:35–12:2, where we read about people who were tortured, imprisoned, stoned, cut in two, and much more, for their faith. The words of this song are as follows:

> *We're pilgrims on the journey*
> *Of the narrow road,*
> *And those who've gone before us line the way.*
> *Cheering on the faithful, encouraging the weary,*
> *Their lives a stirring testament to God's sustaining grace.*

Surrounded by so great a cloud of witnesses,
Let us run the race not only for the prize,
But as those who've gone before us.
Let us leave to those behind us,
The heritage of faithfulness passed on through godly lives.

After all our hopes and dreams have come and gone,
And our children sift though all we've left behind,
May the clues that they discover, and the memories they uncover,
Become the light that leads them, to the road we each must find.

Chorus:
O may all who come behind us find us faithful,
May the fire of our devotion light their way.
May the footprints that we leave,
Lead them to believe,
And the lives we live inspire them to obey.
O may all who come behind us find us faithful.

That is true significance.

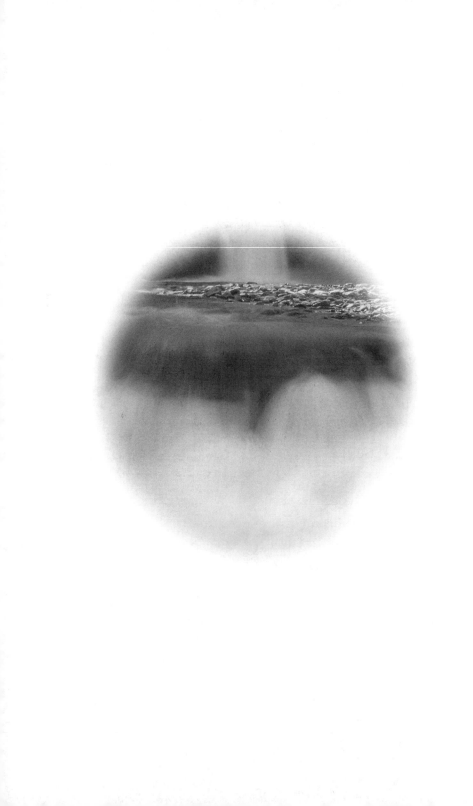

Stay
in the
Moment

For years, Mike Singletary anchored the defense for the Chicago Bears of the National Football League. He was not just your average middle linebacker. He was a warrior; he's been called the greatest middle linebacker to ever play the game. His glare famously intimidated the opposition. Today he is in the NFL Hall of Fame.

Mike is also a committed Christian, and some people had a difficult time understanding how the Christian call to love God and love others could mix with the ferocity required to play NFL football. During an interview before more than two thousand people at the 2004 Super Bowl breakfast, he was asked a very interesting question: "Your commitment to Christ is no secret, but how do you explain the intensity in which you played?"

I loved Mike's answer. He replied: "Early on I realized that the talents and abilities that I have to play football were given to me by God. I also realized that everything I do with my life and in this life must be done for the honor and glory of God.

So when I stepped on that field, I was determined not to rob God of His glory by not using, to the best of my ability, all that He had given me to play football."

What makes Christians different is not what we do, but *why* we do what we do. Because we're going to meet the King, we approach this life differently—with the King's values and perspective. This translates life into incredible opportunities and moments of impact.

While we're on our journey toward heaven, God wants us to make a difference right here, right now in this very moment. He wants us to live with a sense of "spiritual split vision"— one eye focused on where we are going and the other eye on where we are now. In fact, we allow our vision of heaven to determine how and what we do with where we are at any given moment.

GOD CAN USE YOU NOW

Recently someone asked me if there was anything that I wish I had done differently in the past twenty-five years. *Anything?* I have an entire grocery list! But near the very top is this one lesson: *Stay in the moment—look for ways for God to use you to accomplish His purposes each day.*

Throughout my life and ministry, I have struggled with impatience. I tend always to be dreaming about what I want to do in the future. This can sometimes result in my "missing the moment." I'm grateful for the many wonderful things God has done through my life and ministry, but I can see so many opportunities I had for even greater, deeper usefulness for Christ and His kingdom if I hadn't been so preoccupied with accomplishing the next thing.

And then I remember a three-year "moment" early on in my ministry.

At the very beginning of this period, I had an experience that proved to be prophetic. One morning I went to pray at a nearby park. I sat by a small pond, and as I prayed about the exciting opportunity before us, I took a rock and tossed it into the water. As I watched the ripples spread across the pond's surface, it was as if the Lord impressed on my mind, *Crawford, you concentrate on the depth of your relationship with Me, and I will take care of the extent and impact of your ministry.*

WE ARE CALLED TO ACCOMPLISH HIS PURPOSES WHERE WE ARE.

God kept bringing me back to this message during that three-year period. When we lost a baby girl who died just two hours after she was born, we held on to His promise. When we faced unmet expectations and relational disappointments, we remembered His call to us. When tough times made me feel like I was trying to run in sand, we clung to Him.

During that time I did not feel very fruitful. I wondered whether we needed to seek another opportunity. But God taught us to stay in the moment, to do right no matter what, to look for ways He could use us. I gained the conviction that I should never leave a ministry because I'm unhappy—I should respond to the positive call of God in my life.

Now I look back from the vantage point of a few decades and see that season in a different light. I view it as the most significant time in my life and ministry. Most of the convictions I share in this book, for example, were forged during those three years. God taught me how to respond out of sheer obedience and faith, despite how I felt. It was far more fruitful than I ever imagined. To a large degree, that period represents the foundation for our approach to ministry.

God has not called us to minister where we are not. We are called to accomplish His purposes *where we are.* And sometimes our most significant ministry takes place during times of hardship and challenge. Of course we don't realize it at the moment, but when we look back we are amazed at what God did in us and through us during those times of challenge and adversity. God does not always allow us to immediately see the fruit of our labors and struggles. But our struggles are heaven's fertilizer that will produce fruitful yield.

"AND IF I PERISH, I PERISH"

Along our journey toward heaven, God will orchestrate events and circumstances so that He can use us to accomplish His purposes. Sometimes we forget that we are on a divine assignment in this life. Queen Esther in the Old Testament had to be reminded of this. Through an amazing and miraculous chain of events, Esther, a Jewish woman, married Ahasuerus, the king of Persia. The king adored his young, beautiful queen, and God gave Esther great favor and influence.

But a deadly storm was brewing. Haman, one of the king's powerful officials, despised the Jews living in Persia and developed a scheme to annihilate them. When Esther's Jewish uncle, Mordecai, discovered the plot, he told his niece. At first Esther was hesitant to use her influence. She probably didn't want to put in jeopardy her prominence, her influence, or her luxurious lifestyle. She also was afraid she might lose her life if she violated the strict protocol regarding visiting the king (Esther 4:9–12).

Mordecai responded by saying this was not the time to worry about position and protocol. She was the queen, the king favored her, and she was the last line of defense for the preservation of the Jews. Then he confronted her with the God factor

—the real reason why she was in such a unique position. "Do not imagine that you in the king's palace can escape any more than all the Jews. For if you remain silent at this time, relief and deliverance will arise for the Jews from another place and you and your father's house will perish. *And who knows whether you have not obtained royalty for such a time as this?*" (Esther 4:13–14).

That last line touched Esther's heart. She decided she needed to do what must be done, no matter what, "and if I perish, I perish." She went on and told her husband about Haman's plot, and the Jews were saved from massacre. It is a wonderful story of God's sovereignty and how He moves in the lives of normal people like you and me to accomplish His purposes.

It is no accident that we are where we are. Life just doesn't happen. God wants us to view and use every location in our lives as an opportunity, an "outlet," to express His purposes and influence people for Christ and His kingdom. The prominence, favor, and position that God gives to us is not meant to build monuments to ourselves and to our status in this life. God is all about using us to accomplish something eternal, right now during our moment in history.

WITH EVERY LAST BREATH

So the question is: What are you doing with your moment? What are you doing with your "right now"?

I've already mentioned Bill Bright. For more than fifty years he gave leadership to Campus Crusade for Christ, an incredible worldwide movement that grew to more than twenty-seven thousand staff serving around the world. Campus Crusade is the visible expression of the purpose and passion that gripped the heart of Bill Bright. He had a deep, profound love for Jesus Christ, and he was completely committed to fulfilling the Great Commission (Matthew 28:18–20).

He often said, "The greatest thing that has ever happened to me is coming to know Jesus Christ. So the greatest thing I can do for others is to introduce them to my Savior." He was gripped with the desire and vision to give every person in the world an opportunity to know the Savior and experience His love. He gave himself tirelessly and completely to this calling —whether it was sharing Christ with a hotel maid or sitting in a conference room outlining a strategy to introduce millions to the Savior.

Bill Bright knew he wasn't going to live forever, so he used every last moment—and literally every last breath God gave him—to follow His call. During the last few years of his life, he was stricken by pulmonary fibrosis, a debilitating and fatal lung disease. His travel was restricted, and eventually he was bedridden. But even from his bed, he supervised the production of dozens of books and other media projects. He wrote articles and letters. He called staff members and others to encourage them and he prayed for them. Did he ever pray! He prayed for the lost, he prayed for pastors and Christian leaders, he prayed for world leaders. He was determined to use every possible moment to further God's kingdom.

And then, surrounded by his dear wife, Vonette, his family, and a few friends, and after listening to them sing some of his favorite hymns, (no doubt enjoying every note and word he heard), he slipped into the arms of the One whom he had told millions about. The journey ended. He is at home.

God, of course, uses all of us in different ways; not all of us are called to give our life toward evangelizing millions, as Dr. Bright did so generously for so long. *But God does want each of us to take our moment, our unique position and circumstances, and infect time with eternity by pouring the values of heaven into the journey.*

WHAT GREAT CHRISTIANS DO WELL

I have long been interested in people like Bill Bright—believers whom God uses in a great way. As I have studied the Scriptures and read biographies and interacted with such women and men, I've observed that they have several things in common. These character qualities are very obvious and pronounced in their approach to their lives, to their journey on earth, and to the assignments God had given to them.

First, they have been characterized by *brokenness.* Brokenness has to do with the permanent sense of needing God—the realization that we cannot do anything in our own efforts to please Him. God undoes us so that He can remake us. He doesn't want us to trust in our abilities, education, experiences, talents, or gifts. He will use all of these things—but everything He gives us He wants us to use in ways that glorify Him.

We ought to be consciously aware that we are in desperate need of God every second of every day. He will allow us to experience failure and defeat and suffering and trial to see the terrible sinfulness in our hearts, so that He can reveal that He is all-sufficient. In the Old Testament, the prophet Isaiah saw a vision of God's glory that left him reeling and declaring, "Woe is me, for I am ruined!" (Isaiah 6:5). Moses lived in exile on the backside of the desert for forty years, stripped of self-reliance and self-importance before he was commissioned to deliver God's people from bondage (Exodus 3 and 4). Before David became the greatest king that Israel ever had, he literally ran for his life and lived as a fugitive for sixteen years, hiding in caves and learning what it meant to trust in God and God alone (Psalm 40:4–5).

For each of us the message is the same. In the words of A. W. Tozer, "Before God can use us greatly, He hurts us deeply." This is brokenness. It is not simply an intellectual acknowledgment that we need God; it is a life that embraces the primacy of God in all things.

*G*OD DOESN'T DO MORE THROUGH US BECAUSE OFTENTIMES WE'RE NOT SERIOUS ABOUT SPENDING TIME IN HIS PRESENCE.

Second, those who have been greatly used of God have been characterized by what I call *uncommon communion with God*. I am not referring to prayer in general, or even to our daily prayer time. I'm talking about the discipline of intentionally pouring out our hearts to God in believing prayer in order to secure His divine resources to accomplish the tasks He has assigned to us.

It is a picture of Moses, who frequented the "tent of meeting" to hear from God concerning what He wanted him to do (Exodus 33:7–11). It is a picture of Jesus spending forty days in the wilderness before beginning His public ministry and then frequently getting away to pray throughout the remainder of His life on earth.

Jonathan Edwards was an American pastor and theologian in the mid-1700s whose writings still influence pastors and theologians in the early twenty-first century. But when I was reading George Marsden's fascinating biography on Edwards, I was struck by the man's extraordinary daily devotion to God. Describing the routine Edwards maintained each day, Marsden writes, "Edwards usually rose at four or five in the morning in order to spend thirteen hours in his study. . . . Throughout the day, his goal was to remain constantly with a sense of living in the presence of God, as difficult as that might be. Often he added secret days of fasting and additional prayers."[4]

God doesn't do more through us because oftentimes we're not serious about spending time in His presence. When we face problems, we typically turn to our contacts, our resources, and our experts. We call a meeting to sort things out. We act as if the wisdom and insight of bright, wise people is all we require, when in reality we desperately need God. If we are serious about reflecting the values of eternity along the journey, then we need to make spending time with the Author of eternity the calling of our lives.

LIVING OBEDIENCE

Another attribute of those who have been greatly used by God is *radical, immediate obedience.* The nineteenth-century evangelist Dwight Moody would often say, "If God told me to jump out of a window, I would do it." Of course God does not tell anyone to commit suicide; Moody's point was that the most important thing he could ever do was to completely obey God. Because of this faith and obedience, God knew that He could trust Moody—and trust Moody He did. Moody died over a hundred years ago, but his life and ministry continues to bear fruit to this very day through Moody Church in Chicago, Moody Bible Institute, and the godly legacies of those who surrendered their lives to Christ through his ministries.

More recently, two young graduates of "Mr. Moody's school" stood as shining examples of what they called "sacred surrender." Gary and Bonnie Witherall sensed a call to go to minister in Lebanon early in 2001—before 9/11 but at a time of increased Middle Eastern tensions. Family and friends questioned their decision. Bonnie herself had thought, "I'll go anywhere *but* the Middle East!" But a number of "circumstances" came together to convince them to serve their Lord in dangerous southern Lebanon, spreading (as Gary put it) Christ's "message of love and forgiveness." God told this couple to go, and they went. It was that simple.

On the morning of November 21, 2002, Bonnie went as usual to open up the clinic where she worked with poor, pregnant Palestinian women from a local refugee camp. A gunman, who evidently had been waiting for her, shot her at close range. Bonnie Penner Witherall, at thirty-one, was welcomed into the embrace of Jesus—in the ultimate surrender.

When we *don't* obey, we stray off course. When we ignore what we have been told to do and make bad choices, we shouldn't be surprised when we end up in the wrong places. This was the basic difference between King Saul and King David. Paul crystallizes this distinction in Acts 13:22: "And after He had removed him [Saul], He raised up David to be their king, concerning whom He also testified and said, 'I have found David, the son of Jesse, a man after My heart who will do all My will.'"

It is not our intentions that make the difference, but our *acts of obedience* that draw the attention and resources of heaven to impact our moments in history. God smiles on us and the work of our hands when we give ourselves to completely doing what He has called us to do.

Many believers today have barely heard of Corrie ten Boom, but her story is one of the most extraordinary of the twentieth century. An unmarried, middle-aged daughter of a watchmaker in Holland, Corrie and her family were caught up in the catastrophic events of World War II. She relied on her strong faith in Christ to endure the horrors of the Ravensbruck concentration camp. When God miraculously spared her life, she dedicated the rest of her days to telling others about Him.

In her book *Tramp for the Lord*, she tells of a memorable encounter after speaking in a church in Munich, Germany, in 1947. She had spoken on God's forgiveness, because she knew that this was a message that the defeated and broken Germans needed to hear. When she finished speaking, she noticed a man coming forward to speak with her.

"One moment I saw the overcoat and the brown hat; the next, a blue uniform and a visored cap with its skull and crossbones," she writes. "It came back [to me] with a rush; the huge room with its harsh overhead lights; the pathetic pile of dresses and shoes in the center of the floor; the shame of walking naked past this man . . . The place was Ravensbruck and the man who was making his way forward had been a guard—one of the most cruel guards."

The former guard did not recognize Corrie, but he told her that after the war ended he had become a Christian. "I know that God has forgiven me for the cruel things I did there, but I would like to hear it from your lips as well, Fraulein." He reached out his hand and asked, "Will you forgive me?"

Corrie felt frozen as she decided what to do. She didn't feel any forgiveness for this man, but she knew forgiveness was an act of obedience, for the Scriptures tell us to forgive those who have injured us. So she took his hand, and "as I did, an incredible thing took place. The current started in my shoulder, raced down my arm, sprang into our joined hands. And then this healing warmth seemed to flood my whole being, bringing tears to my eyes. 'I forgive you, brother!' I cried. 'With all my heart.'"

"For a long moment we grasped each other's hands, the former guard and the former prisoner. I had never known God's love so intensely as I did then."[5]

Heroes of the faith like Corrie ten Boom and Bonnie Witherall don't go through life knowing all the ways God will use them. But they *do* know that God has a plan for their journey, and they need to give themselves completely to Him and what He wants to do through them.

This life is our one and only opportunity to live for eternity. What we do with what God places before us is in our hands. We can either pour eternity into our timeline (Ephesians 5:15–17) or we can ignore the divine appointments and opportunities by choosing a self-determined life.

The choices begin now—in this moment.

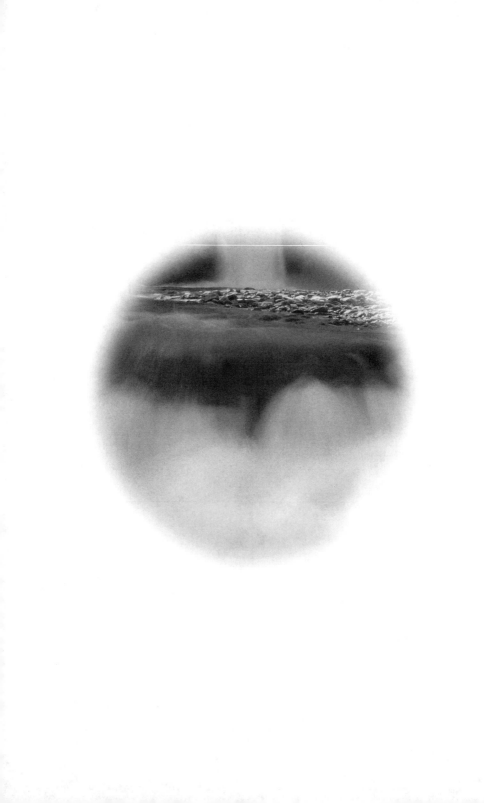

Be
Fervent

Remember the California wildfires awhile back?

They gobbled up thousands of acres of forest. Families were forced to flee their homes; TV showed images of walls of flame looming behind villages. But what really stunned me was the video footage taken from a helicopter—the tape panned over miles and miles of scorched, charred remains of what once were houses and lush green trees.

I had a similar experience a few years ago when much of the Southeast was battered with torrential rain. The streams, rivers, and lakes couldn't hold the massive volume of water. There were widespread reports of flooding. But it was particularly devastating in some of the communities in southern Georgia. And once again, when I saw the video footage taken from a small aircraft, my heart ached for the suffering and loss these people were experiencing. Houses were literally immersed in water. Pets and household items floated away. Caskets from a local cemetery drifted downstream.

These panoramic pictures painted a portrait of the comprehensive nature of the damage. They also served as a compelling and convincing call to compassion, to help those who were suffering. And many responded. People prayed, sent food and clothes, provided temporary housing, and volunteered to help repair damaged property.

Whether it is fires in southern California, floods in southern Georgia, a tsunami in Asia, or thousands of lives lost because of terrorist attacks in New York City—to witness the scope of the wreckage, the sheer mass of the tragedy, breaks your heart and opens your eyes.

If only we could view the human plight in the same way. If only we could see what God sees.

Every second of every day, millions of lives are devastated. Right before our eyes, those without Christ, those who don't know Him or have turned from Him, are destroying themselves. Think of people you know—a friend, neighbor, associate, or family member. Do you see their faces? When they close their eyes in death, that's it. They are forever lost.

Do we care—as God cares?

Think about it. God paid the ultimate, severe, sacrificial price to forgive our sins, buy us back, and to change our destiny. Ponder and meditate on these familiar words in John 3:16–18:

> *For God so loved the world, that He gave His only begotten Son, that whoever believes in Him should not perish, but have eternal life. For God did not send the Son into the world to judge the world, but that the world should be saved through Him. He who believes in Him is not judged; he who does not believe has been judged already, because he has not believed in the name of the only begotten Son of God.*

This is the message that is the heart and core identity of every follower of Jesus Christ. We have believed and have been given the gift of eternal life. We are forgiven and forever His, and we will be with Him forever (John 14:1–3). But what about those around us? On our journey toward heaven we come across others every day who are headed in the opposite direction. They are lost, and many of them don't know it. But we do.

It's like a small child with a life-threatening illness. He's not aware of the seriousness of his condition, but those who love him understand, and they give him the attention and care he needs in order to save his life.

I believe we have become too laid-back and casual in sharing the good news with others. We approach people as if a relationship with Christ is nice, but not necessary. Of course we wouldn't admit this, but in our desire for others to embrace our message, we forget that life on this side of the grave is terminal. We forget that what a person decides to do with Jesus in this life is the determining factor with regard to his eternal destiny. What we have to share is beyond good advice; it is the cure for the devastating disease of sin, and it places us on the road toward heaven.

He HAS NOT TOLD US WHEN OUR TIME IS UP; HE HAS ONLY TOLD US WHAT HE WANTS US TO DO WHILE WE HAVE TIME.

Of course we should be strategic, winsome, and relevant when we present the good news to others. We should be loving and patient. We ought to present the gospel wrapped in words and a context that will appeal to our audience. But we also should not lose a sense of urgency as we present the gospel to others. Every encounter you have with a person who does not know Christ might be the last opportunity that person has to surrender his life to Him. Tomorrow is not guaranteed. All we have is right now.

"I Will Build My Church"

Why do so many Christians lose their sense of urgency in telling others about Christ? I think the first reason is that *it is easy to lose sight of what God is doing in human history and how we fit into this plan.*

Have you ever thought about the fact that, at some point in your future, time as you know it will end? Either you will die and pass out of your earthly existence, or our Lord will return and we will go to be with Him. Only God knows when either will take place. He has not told us when our time is up; He has only told us what He wants us to do while we have time. He wants us to stay focused on our moment in history and to use this moment to participate in accomplishing His mission. Right now God is going about the business of building His church. That's the point of Matthew 16:13–18:

> *Now when Jesus came into the district of Caesarea Philippi, He began asking His disciples, saying, "Who do people say that the Son of Man is?" And they said, "Some say John the Baptist; and others, Elijah; but still others, Jeremiah, or one of the prophets." He said to them, "But who do you say that I am?" And Simon Peter answered and said, "Thou art the Christ, the Son of the living God." And Jesus answered and said to him, "Blessed are you, Simon Bar-jona, because flesh and blood did not reveal this to you, but My Father who is in heaven. And I also say to you that you are Peter, and upon this rock I will build My church; and the gates of Hades shall not overpower it."*

Several observations need to be made about Jesus' profound declaration in this passage. First, *Jesus' authority is anchored in the fact that He is "the Christ, the Son of the living God."*

By this time, the disciples had been up close and personal with Jesus for perhaps as long as two years. They had heard His messages, seen His miracles, witnessed the confrontations, and now it was their turn to answer the most important question of all time: *Who is Jesus?* Peter, no doubt answering for his colleagues, said, "Thou art the Christ, the Son of the living God."

Jesus is not a Christ; He is *the* Christ. *Christ* is the Greek transliteration of *Messiah,* which means "the Anointed One." He is God in flesh, the Son of the living God, and He is God's focal point of human history and His mission in the world. There is no other deliverer or source of deliverance from the penalty and power of sin than Jesus Christ (Acts 4:12). He has neither rival, nor equal (Colossians 1:13–20).

He is not merely a man among men; He is the everlasting God-man. You cannot even mention His name in the same sentence with the most outstanding personalities in human history. He is not one of them. He is their Creator, hopefully their Redeemer, and one day their Judge. Jesus is Lord.

Second, *Jesus Christ is not only the head of the church, but the church also belongs to Him.* He said, "I will build *My* church." This has enormous implications concerning how the church of Jesus Christ functions in the world. Because we are Christ's church, we are not free to function in any way we choose. We follow our leader, our commander in chief. He owns our lives and this collective living organism called the church. As the owner He can do with His church whatever He pleases.

By *church,* I don't just mean the church you belong to. I mean all of those who have placed their faith in Jesus Christ. Whether you are Chinese, Japanese, Rwandan, Brazilian, Iraqi, Israeli, Irish, American, or anything else, if you have trusted Christ, then you are a member of the family of God—His church. The very word, *church*, is descriptive of God's mission. Church comes from the Greek word *ecclesia,* which means "called out." God is calling out a people for Himself.

THE VOICE FROM HOME

Third, *this declaration clearly depicts our Lord's mission in human history.* Jesus said, "I *will* build My church." God is building, expanding, and multiplying His church until time is no more. He is doing this both quantitatively and qualitatively.

By *qualitatively,* I mean He wants the members of His church to look more and more like Him so that the unbelieving world sees Christ in and through the members of His church (Ephesians 3:14–19; 4:13–16). He leaves His church in the world so that we will look like Him to the world (Ephesians 2:19–22). In the process, we are overcoming sin, experiencing holiness, and demonstrating what a citizen of heaven looks like.

My ministry sometimes takes me to other countries. Sometimes I feel like I am the only American in a particular city. So if I happen to hear a voice with that distinctive American flavor, I am drawn to it. Although I am in another country and in a different culture, I recognize that voice from home.

The church of Jesus Christ is God's delegation from heaven. It is the "voice from home." It is calling us to live lives worthy of the Savior and of the journey. The church is a visible demonstration of the transforming power of Jesus Christ.

But our Savior is also building his church *quantitatively.* He is adding numbers to His church by reclaiming the lives that have been snatched by sin and Satan. Here the church is viewed as an army that is in a hurry. General Jesus, through His church, is on a mission.

The last line of Matthew 16:18 reads, "And the gates of Hades shall not overpower [the church]." Unfortunately this translation makes it appear as if "the gates of Hades" is the aggressor. But there is an alternative rendering in the Greek text that I prefer, and I think it better fits the context. Allow me to paraphrase: "The gates of Hades shall not be able to withstand the aggressive onslaught of the church." We are making a holy, intentional assault on the kingdom of darkness in the name of our everlasting, risen Lord and Savior Jesus Christ. We are His battering ram to break through the barriers of darkness and set free the captives of sin.

The church is not some club, society, or even charitable organization. The church is a living, dynamic movement that carries with it the heart of God on an urgent mission to reach and deliver lost people before time runs out.

Leaving—Not Losing

There is another reason I believe we lose our sense of urgency in the world today: *Our focus and our hearts drift away from the center of Christianity, Jesus Christ.* Any drift away from Christ essentially leads to warped thinking about the Christian life.

This was a problem with the church in Ephesus. In Revelation 2:1–5 we find Jesus dictating a letter to John to be sent this church. Look closely at what Jesus said:

> "To the angel of the church in Ephesus write: The One who holds the seven stars in His right hand, the One who walks among the seven golden lampstands, says this: 'I know your deeds and your toil and perseverance, and that you cannot endure evil men, and you put to the test those who call themselves apostles, and they are not, and you found them to be false; and you have perseverance and have endured for My name's sake, and have not grown weary.

But I have this against you, that you have left your first love. Remember therefore from where you have fallen, and repent and do the deeds you did at first; or else I am coming to you, and will remove your lampstand out of its place—unless you repent.'"

Apparently the Ephesians were living exemplary lives. Jesus praised them for right behavior—He recognized them for their deeds, toil, perseverance, and for not enduring evil men. He also commended them for both understanding and practicing the truth. No heresy there. These were people we might today admire as "Bible believing."

Now I must admit that when I first read this passage a number of years ago, I thought to myself, "This sounds good to me. They are living right and their heads are screwed on right when it comes to understanding the Word of God. What problem could Jesus possibly have with these people?"

But there was a serious problem, and it's one that we see in many of Christ's followers today. In fact, the cause of Christ is hamstrung because of this problem. Jesus clearly states the problem in verse 4: "But I have this against you, that you have left your first love." In this stinging indictment, Jesus reminds us that authentic, biblical Christianity has everything to do with a relationship with Jesus Christ.

There are three words in verse 4 that drip with implications. First, Jesus says, "you have *left* your first love." He didn't say that they lost it; he said that they *left* it. And there is a big difference between losing something and leaving something.

I'll never forget waking up one morning several years ago with great excitement about what was on my schedule for that day. That morning I had a meeting scheduled with other leaders to discuss an innovative plan to reach a certain group of people with the gospel. Then I would be traveling to a city where I would be presenting the gospel at a large gathering.

I was thrilled with the wonderful opportunities before me. I rushed out of the house carrying my bags and my briefcase, but as I drove to the office I had this nagging feeling that I had forgotten something. And then I remembered—I had left my wallet on my dresser. I didn't lose it; I knew exactly where it was. But in my enthusiasm and excitement over good, God-sanctioned opportunities, I left something very important and essential. I was driving without identification.

Some of us are living the Christian life without proper identification. Jesus has, in effect, been left on the dresser and we are running around trying to impress people with what we believe and how we behave.

FIRST THINGS FIRST

Jesus also says, "You have left your *first* love." The word *first* here doesn't simply refer to a list of priorities, but to *the* priority of our lives—that which establishes and gives order to everything else we do. It is what our lives are built on, and it gives meaning and eternal value to what we do and how we live.

Our relationship with Jesus Christ is primary and preeminent to all that we are and all that we do. He is first and foremost. We are defined by our relationship with Him.

My relationship with my wife, Karen, is a picture of how my relationship with Christ should be my highest priority. My relationship with Karen is the core human relationship that I have in this life. She is first and foremost, she has access to my life, and in many respects my choices and decisions are made against the backdrop of this relationship.

It would be easy for me to become so consumed by the things I do—the meetings I attend, speaking engagements, the books and articles I write—and neglect my most important human relationship. But I only have one Karen. When we married, we committed our lives completely and fully to each other until separated by death. I don't want to get so caught up in what I am doing that good activities and opportunities become like a seductive mistress pulling me away from Karen, my first and foremost love.

Yet even more important, when I committed my life to Jesus Christ, He became my core, primary relationship. If I do not intentionally nurture this relationship, my passion is drawn away from Christ to other things. And I don't necessarily mean bad things. Just as the Christians at Ephesus were more passionate about what they believed and how they lived than they were about Jesus, we too can love our theological insights and positions, our knowledge of the Bible, and our codes of conduct more than we love Jesus.

LOVER OF MY SOUL

That leads me to the third word in the Revelation 2 passage: "You have left your first *love.*" The word *love* is the familiar Greek word *agape.* I think in our desire to have a nice, easy, memorable definition of *agape* we may have trivialized its meaning. We say that agape is God's unconditional love. Although this is accurate, there is so much more.

Trying to define agape is sort of like trying to define God's holiness. At a certain point there is a disconnect. Just as the finite human mind cannot begin to fathom the proactive purity (holiness) of God, our hearts and minds cannot begin to understand and appreciate the severe love of God for us.

Ephesus had been a cesspool of immorality and idol wor-
shipers when the apostle Paul showed up (Acts 19). And many
of what would become respectable "church folk" had been
wrapped up in unimaginable sin. Through the preaching of
the apostle Paul, the love of God through Christ had pursued
them, caught them, cleaned them up, given
them a home in heaven, and provided them
with a mission in this life. Jesus Christ had
delivered their souls and changed their lives.

But they forgot. It's as if Jesus had to remind them, "You have forgotten that it was
the love of God through Me that ran you
down. Your correct theology and right behavior didn't save you—I did."

It's like a marriage that has grown cold.
There is an emotional distance in the relationship. Oh, the husband and wife still live
together, go to work, take care of the house,
and raise the children. But they have taken the
relationship for granted. They may live in a
big, lovely house and drive late-model cars,
but truthfully they were happier when all they had was each
other. Now all of the other "stuff" has gotten in the way.
Their hearts are divided and the fire is dwindling.

*I*F WE WANT
TO MAKE JESUS
CHRIST THE
CENTRAL
FIGURE IN
OUR LIVES,
THEN WE HAVE
TO REMEMBER,
REPENT, AND
REDO.

It's common for Christians to go through a period of "leaving your first love" a few years after they come to faith. You may
still be active in your church—in fact, you may be a pastor or a
full-time Christian worker—but something inside is missing:

• You spend less and less time in God's Word, and when
  you do the passages seem to lack the passion and imme-
  diacy they once had.

- You don't talk with God throughout the day as you once did. In fact, it's hard to remember when you last prayed with any kind of conviction.
- The sermons that once seemed so powerful and personal now seem to run together in your mind, and it is rare that you are able to pay attention longer than five or ten minutes.
- You begin to feel stretched, like you're going through day after day and week after week relying on your own talents, and you have little sense of God empowering you.
- The things of the world—your interests, your career, your entertainment, even your relationships—capture your thoughts much more than thoughts of heaven.
- You just don't feel close to God like you once did.

IGNITING OUR PASSION

Fortunately, Jesus tells the Ephesians—and anyone who has left his first love—how to get things back in line. Verse 5 says, "Remember therefore from where you have fallen, and repent and do the deeds you did at first." If we want to make Jesus Christ the central figure in our lives, then we have to *remember, repent,* and *redo.*

He tells us to remember from where we have fallen. Push the rewind button and refresh our memories. We need to remember the beauty and simplicity of our commitment to the person of Christ.

You know how it was. Remember? You didn't know anything about theology or the Bible. You just knew that the greatest thing imaginable just happened to you. You were clean, forgiven, peace flooded your soul, and you were engulfed in the love of Christ. You just couldn't thank Him enough for changing your life and giving you a home in heaven. And you wanted to share the love of Jesus with everyone you knew.

Then Jesus says to repent, which literally means to change your mind. Jesus is calling us to change our minds about how we approach the Christian life. This first involves examining your heart and confessing to God anything that has kept you from Him. Make up your mind that you are going to be defined by your love relationship with Jesus Christ. Everything else will extend from that relationship. Turn from trusting in yourself, your insights, and even the truths that you know. Make it your holy ambition to be known as a follower and lover of Jesus.

The church of Jesus Christ needs to repent of our misplaced passion. We are sending to the world a mixed message. We come across as if we love our causes more than we love Christ. We may be right in our perspective on an issue or a cause, but some of us are so consumed and obsessed by our issues and causes that Jesus has been lost. We present to the world a tainted Christianity and a confused gospel. And what many unbelievers really hear and see from us is this message: "Unless you agree with our view on these issues, you can't enter the kingdom of God."

Jesus must be first and foremost in our perspective on the Christian life, in our process of living the Christian life, and in our presentation of authentic Christianity to others. Jesus is calling us to stand back and evaluate our lives against His lordship and honestly repent of anything and everything else that has encroached upon His rightful place.

Finally, Jesus says, "Do the deeds you did at first." Retrace your steps, go back to the beginning, simplify your Christianity. Rediscover the beauty and the wonder of that initial love relationship with Jesus.

When was the last time you spent several hours with Jesus —reading the Scriptures, praying, talking with Him? When was the last time you spent even one hour with Him? If you have not, is it any wonder that your passion for Christ and for His mission here on earth has grown cold?

For years Karen and I have spoken at hundreds of marriage conferences across the country. One purpose of these conferences is to show couples that their relationship with Christ is the key to forming the kind of lasting marriage they desire. By the end of these conferences, I always enjoy the opportunity to talk with many of these couples who walk up to tell me how their lives have been changed. What strikes me is that often I hear the same type of story.

A couple arrives at the conference on Friday night, and for a while they wonder why they are even there. But as the weekend progresses, not only do they enjoy the conference, but they rediscover the joy of each other's company. For many couples it's their first time away together for a weekend in many years. Often one will say, "This is giving me the chance to see the man I married," or "We had fun again, the way we did when we were just married."

But not only do these couples rediscover the "first love" of their spouse, but more important, they also connect again with God. Many have been Christians for years but realize they have drifted away from their most important first love. As they learn to build their home on biblical principles, they begin to regain a love for God's Word, and they desire to spend more time with Him. They return home with a renewed sense of God's presence in their lives, a strong hunger for a deeper walk with Christ, and a sense of urgency about reaching out to friends and loved ones.

We don't have time for distractions. God is on an urgent

mission that He wants to accomplish through us—and His mission is all about Jesus. God wants you to see what He sees concerning the truth of the human condition. But we will never see it until our total focus is on Jesus. When we focus on Jesus, He ignites the passion in our souls for Him, and He ignites our passion for His mission in the world.

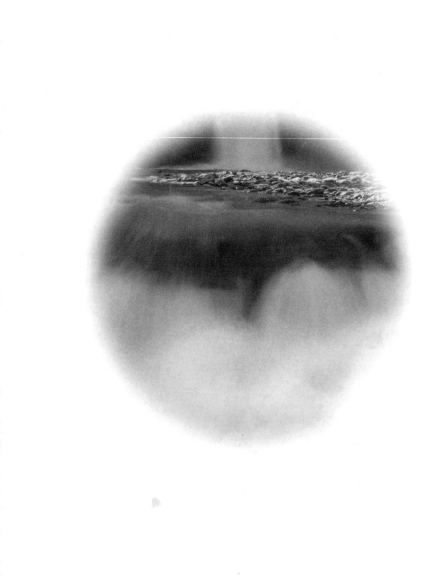

Spiritual Footprints

I remember sitting in front of the television as a child, spellbound by the performances of Sammy Davis Jr. He was enormously talented as a dancer, singer, comedian, and actor. He performed with an energy and magnetic charisma that sprang from natural talent, not technological spectacle or electronic enhancement. And he became a standard, a model for other entertainers to follow.

One of his most-committed disciples was Gregory Hines, the award-winning entertainer who starred both in film and on stage. When Davis died some years ago from complications from throat cancer, Hines paid tribute to his beloved mentor during the memorial service.

Hines described how he and his brothers, when they were kids, used to sneak into Harlem's Apollo Theater to watch Sammy Davis Jr. perform with his uncles. He was inspired to model his own performances after those of Davis—who eventually helped him get started in the business. Through the years a deep affection and bond developed between them.

And then Hines told a moving story about visiting Davis a few weeks before he passed away. Hines knew the disease was terminal, and he wanted to say thank you and good-bye to the man who had done so much to shape his career.

Even if a person doesn't intend to leave a legacy, he or she will.

When Hines walked into the house, he was struck by the toll the cancer had taken. Always a slight man, Davis was even more frail and emaciated. The cancer had robbed the singer of his voice, so Hines did most of the talking. He told Davis how much he had meant to him, thanked him for all he had done for him. He said good-bye and affectionately kissed Davis on the cheek and got up to leave.

As Hines walked toward the door he heard the shuffling of feet. He turned and saw Davis behind him. The mentor had one last message, one last charge, to give his student.

Davis pretended as if he had a basketball in his hands and passed it to Hines. That gesture said it all: "I have gone as far as I can. This is the end of the line for me, so what I have I give to you. The ball is in your hands. You have to take it to a time that I cannot see." Gregory Hines left the house determined to do all that he could to keep, preserve, and build on the legacy.

I am moved by that story because it is a compelling picture of the nature and cycle of influence God has called all of us to have upon others. As followers of Jesus Christ, we are on our journey toward heaven—our home, and our ultimate reward. But long after we are gone, until the Lord returns, heaven's work continues. And those we influence—friends, family members, and associates—continue to live. They go to a time that we cannot experience or see. Every life is a transition to another era.

The truth of the matter is that to live means to influence. Even if a person doesn't intend to leave a legacy, he or she will. That issue is not even on the table. Every life is a personal story about destiny that is read by those who know the person. We are all telling a story.

Think about that. Each day you are shaping your legacy. Your values and convictions, and how you live them out through your words and your actions, will influence everyone around you. If you are a parent, this is especially sobering because your children will grow up to be like you in ways you can hardly comprehend.

When we die, our work is complete. It is finished; we can't do it over again. The question is: What kind of legacy have you left the next generation?

WEAR YOUR WORK BOOTS

My friend John Oliver, professor of homilitics at Reformed Seminary in Charlotte, North Carolina, points out that there is an important distinction between *history* and *heritage*. History is what has happened, while heritage is what we learn from (and decide to do about) that history. To live means to have history. Each tick of a clock is to experience history. But our calling is to create a spiritual heritage. That's a different matter.

A spiritual heritage is a timeless treasure. It is a historical record of our relationship with God and the application of His eternal truth during our journey toward heaven. It is a record of our response to God and the choices and decisions we have made in light of our relationship with Him.

Heritage is hard to cultivate in the church today. If there is one thing that grieves me, it is that we have developed a brand of Christianity that is self-centered, that works against giving ourselves to others and passing on a godly legacy. We have gotten so obsessed with our perceived need to be happy, prosperous Christians that many of us no longer hear the call of Calvary to lay down our lives and give ourselves completely to Him and to the cause that is bigger than ourselves.

Some years ago a friend said to me, "Crawford, if you are going to leave your footprints in the sands of time, then you're going to have to wear work boots." I want my work boots to leave a deep impression, so that future generations will be able to clearly see my steps and follow the path I have tramped. Chances are that when I die I will not have much money or property to pass along to my children or grandchildren. So I want to pass on a lasting spiritual heritage.

On a table across the room from me is a photograph of our grandsons Quentin, Myles, and Jaden. Those three little guys probably represent the last generation in our family that will have a physical, emotional connection with me. I hold them and kiss them, tell them I love them, read them stories, play with them, and tell them about Jesus. I pray for them. I want them to know that "Papa" loves them and loves Jesus. I want them to see and feel the love of Jesus through me. I want them to hear the Word of God read with my voice to their hearts.

I am sobered by the thought that I may not live long enough to do the same for their children. But I can leave something that will speak to them when I have gone to be with my Lord. For more than thirty years, on most days I have jotted down a page or two in a journal about my walk with Christ—my thoughts, lessons, feelings, challenges, victories, defeats, etc. These little books serve as a record of my spiritual journey.

When I first started this discipline years ago, I had no thought of sharing what I wrote with anyone else, much less to future generations. It was an important spiritual exercise that charted God's work in my life and served as a tangible source of encouragement to me. But as our children got older I began to realize that what I was writing in those journals was not just for me. It is an important part of their spiritual heritage. It is the record of an imperfect pilgrim struggling to live out an authentic relationship with Christ during his moment in history.

So today when I write in my journal, in the back of my mind I know that this is not just about where I am today. Perhaps my children and grandchildren will face a certain problem or challenge and will need to look down and see a footprint and say, "It looks like Papa has been here. How did he handle this? What did he do right? What did he do wrong? What can we learn from him?"

PRAYER OF A PATRIARCH

Psalm 71 is kind of a journal entry of an old man who wants to finish well and is concerned about his influence on future generations. I guess you could say it is the prayer of a patriarch. No one knows who wrote this anonymous psalm. It is a prayer that has been preserved down through the centuries for our benefit and blessing.

The psalmist speaks to the essence of what we need to focus on if we are going to leave a permanent imprint in the sands of time. With the end of his journey in sight, this old warrior pushes aside all the nonessential stuff of life. He's concerned with what really matters. He has what so many older followers of Christ have: a sense of perspective, the ability to be able to distinguish between what is truly important and what is temporary and passing away.

I saw this in my parents as they aged. But I've also seen the other side—people who hold on to the insignificant to the very end. Their lives are defined by the perishable and peripheral stuff of life. They die, the things they held on to are left behind to wear out and disappear, and their loved ones are left with memories that have no substance.

Not so with the patriarch in Psalm 71. He has four major emphases—three prayer requests and a concluding resolve.

First he prays that God will be his *permanent refuge*. Look at verse 3 and part of verse 6 (NASB): "Be to me a rock of habitation to which I may continually come; You have given commandment to save me, for You are my rock and my fortress . . . By You I have been sustained from my birth."

This is a man who is not confused or conflicted. He has learned through the years (perhaps through painful mistakes) that there is only one place where there is guaranteed deliverance and safety, and that is in the presence of God. He is our hiding place, and there is no such thing as devastation in His presence.

I'm reminded of the day I was playing golf with some friends and we got caught in a torrential downpour. The wind was blowing the rain sideways, and lightning was flashing. We were scared and had to do something quick. We spotted a shelter not too far away and made a mad dash to safety. We all let out a collective sigh of relief, and someone said, "I'm so glad this place is here."

Where do others see you go when you are caught in the storms of life? Is God your place of safety?

When we are in a jam or hit with a crisis, sometimes we turn too quickly to our ingenuity, resources, and contacts. But in the end, resources are limited, and they are not the source of our safety. God wants us to go to Him first; He is our protector. As experienced and well-informed as we may be, and as concerned and well-intentioned as others may be, no person can guarantee our safety. Others need to see us turning to God as our safety shelter because they will need one too.

RETURN TO THE OLD NEIGHBORHOOD

The patriarch in Psalm 71 also pictures God as his source of stability, "a rock of habitation to which I may continually come." Consistency and predictability are wonderful things. They produce a sense of confidence in our lives—the feeling that certain people or places will always be there. But that's not really true, is it? Places change, buildings are replaced with highways and condominiums, and the people in our lives move on or pass away.

A few years ago I visited the old neighborhood in Newark, New Jersey, where I spent the first twelve years of my life. I hadn't been there in years. I had vivid memories of the apartment building where I once lived.

The closer I got to the neighborhood, the faster my heart beat with excitement. The scenes of my childhood filled my mind. It was 1960 again, and I was ten years old . . . In my mind, it was Saturday and Mom and my sisters were going downtown and Pop and I were leaving the apartment building on our way to a New York Yankees baseball game.

But when I turned onto Wilsey Street, I quickly woke up from my dream. I guess there is something to the saying, "You can't go home again." I barely recognized the old neighborhood. All of the familiar buildings had been torn down, including 83 Wilsey Street where we used to live, and replaced with condominiums. I suppose I should have expected this, but something in me was hoping that this place that represented stability and gave me so many great memories would still be standing.

Our circumstances change, and we are threatened by the volatility of this thing called life. But our anchor holds. We're not shaken—not because we are so strong—it's our God who is unshakable and utterly reliable. When we continually hold our great God up as our place and source of stability, we offer this and future generations what they so desperately need.

I also think of a ritual I began when I left home for college. Every Sunday night I called my parents. Now Pop wasn't much for long phone conversations. After he would hear that I was doing okay, he would hand the phone to Mom, who was more interested in hearing the details.

I looked forward to those Sunday night conversations. As my parents aged, I would call them several times during the week, but there was always something special about that standing Sunday night phone conversation. It was a tradition.

Pop died in 1995 and Mom in 1997. I'll never forget the Sunday evening about two weeks after her funeral. I instinctively picked up the telephone and began dialing her phone number. Then it hit me—Mom was not there. She was gone.

But there is Someone who is always there. He is the everlasting Ancient of Days. No one will ever tear down His fortress, and He will not pass away. Whenever you go to see Him, He is there. He has not moved, nor has He changed. He is the same yesterday, today, and forever. And His stability produces certainty and stability in our lives.

This wonderful, godly model points to God as his source of sustenance when he says, "By Thee I have been sustained from my birth" (v. 6). He is saying, "God, you have kept me alive."

Just as parents are committed to providing what their children need, so our heavenly Father invites His children to come to Him to receive what we need. There is an interesting implication in the phrase "sustained from my birth." This is a statement of confidence. This veteran follower is saying, "The same Someone who has met all of my needs from the moment I was born to this very day will continue to meet my needs until my time on this earth is complete."

This reminds me of something Bill Bright, the founder of Campus Crusade for Christ used to say. He and his wife, Vonette, lived on a modest income and trusted God to meet their needs. He said sometimes people would ask him, "How are you going to make it financially when you get older?" I love his answer: "The same God who has provided will continue to provide."

ARE YOU A "MARVEL"?

The second prayer in Psalm 71 from this wonderful old warrior is to *allow others to see God at work in his life.* I love the way he puts it in verse 7: "I have become a marvel to many; for Thou art my strong refuge."

What a great word picture. People looked at this old guy and shook their heads in wonder and amazement at his spiritual vitality.

This description reminds me of Dr. Stephen Olford, who was one of the world's greatest preachers until he recently passed away at the age of eighty-six. He was founder of the Stephen Olford Center for Biblical Preaching in Memphis, Tennessee, which trains and mentors younger ministers and preachers.

Olford was a delight to be around. He had a fresh and

attractive relationship with Christ. When you visited with him, you were struck by the faith, vision, and enthusiasm of this servant of the cross. The love of Christ just oozed out of the man, and that's the reason why so many younger people were attracted to him.

Another marvel that comes to mind is my old college buddy, Dean Hertzler, who was stricken by amyotrophic lateral sclerosis, better known as ALS or Lou Gehrig's disease. His body deteriorated, and he was confined to a wheelchair. But his faith did not deteriorate—it grew. I called him a few months before he passed away to offer some encouragement, but he ended up encouraging me. He said he was rejoicing in God's goodness to him. Although his voice was weak, I heard strength in his soul—no complaining, no bitterness, just rejoicing. I was amazed at the power of God in and through his life.

At Dean's memorial service, those who helped care for him shared that God used Dean to inspire them in their walk and relationship with Christ. As I listened to their words, I realized that what may be a severe trial or test for us could be a treasure for others. Those close to Dean looked past his physical condition and saw the life of Christ shining from him. Dean tapped into heaven's resources for the strength he needed to face ALS. In the process, he became a marvel to many who expressed that they could tell that God lived in him and shone through him.

REMEMBER!

Third, the patriarch of Psalm 71 *prays to remember.* Look at his heart in verses 17–18 NASB: "O God, You have taught me from my youth, and I still declare Your wondrous deeds. And even when I am old and gray, O God, do not forsake me, until I declare Your strength to this generation, Your power to all who are to come."

When each of our four children went away to college, we went through the same routine. We got the child settled in his or her dorm room. I typically procrastinated because I didn't want to deal with the inevitable good-bye. (Karen and I thought it would get a bit easier to say good-bye with our later children, but no chance.)

Eventually we would walk out to our car, and we would pray together. Then I would kiss and hug my child and whisper three things. "I love you. Remember who you are. No matter what, obey God." And as I drove away with tear-filled eyes, I found myself praying, "Oh, God, help this child to remember what we've taught them—to be faithful to You."

We, too, need to remember. We need to keep it clear and simple. Don't trade in the spiritual jewels for fool's gold. No matter where life takes us, we should be marked by a simple faith in God, obedience to His Word, and faithfulness in implementing His call for our lives. This is the treasure we pass on to future generations.

In verse 18, the old man asks God to remember him, "Even when I am old and gray, O God, do not forsake me," because he wants to "declare Thy strength to this generation, Thy power to all who are to come." He's not asking for recognition or greatness. He's simply asking God to grant him the ability to declare God's fame to this and future generations as long as he has breath. He's saying, "God, I am available to You, I want to stay in the game; I want to be Your mouthpiece. I want my life and my lips to be a declaration of Your greatness."

Too many older followers of Christ shift into neutral at a certain point. They lose the impact of their lives because they buy into the idea that it's time to enter "retirement." They pull back from meaningful ministry involvement with others so that they can spend the bulk of their time working in the garden, playing golf, watching television, and taking an occasional cruise.

The BASIS, THE REASON, FOR OUR PRAISE SHOULD GO BEYOND WHAT GOD DOES FOR US.

Now, there is nothing wrong with any of this, and certainly as we age we don't have the energy to do some of the things we used to do. And we should enjoy life and the fruit of our labors. *But God never gave us permission to stop declaring His strength and power!* Although the scope of our involvement might be reduced, the fire must never go out. This and future generations desperately need to see living trophies of the grace and power of God.

"GOD IS GOOD"

The patriarch ends his journal entry with a resolve to praise God: "I will also praise You with a harp, even Your truth, O my God; to You I will sing praises with the lyre, O Holy One of Israel. My lips will shout for joy when I sing praises to You . . . my tongue also will utter Your righteousness all day long" (vv. 22–24 NASB).

Praise is a disposition of the heart and not just a response to circumstances. To be sure, God's wonderful gifts, like getting an unexpected bonus at work or experiencing healing of a damaged relationship, should cause us to bow in humble gratitude, thanksgiving, and praise to our wonderful God. But the basis, the *reason,* for our praise should go beyond what God does for us. Our praise is tied to our understanding of who God is.

We know that He is consistent. We know that He is good. We know that He loves us. We know that He is committed to us. We know that we are in His hands. This knowledge informs our wills to look past the pain of our circumstances, even with tears rolling down our cheeks, and declare God's goodness and faithfulness in all things.

As I write these words I have just returned from the memorial service of a good friend of mine, J. T. Walker, who died of leukemia. J. T. was only forty-three when he went home. He and his dear wife, Enid, have five children. What an incredible loss.

Before the service I visited with J. T.'s mother. As I walked toward her, I thought, "I can only imagine the pain and anguish of soul this mother must be going through." I said to Mrs. Walker, "I am so sorry."

I will never forget her response. With tear-filled eyes she said, "God is good. He is in charge, and my son is in a better place." This was not a cliché. This woman of God had walked with God for many years, and she understood that this bitter, painful experience did not change the character of God. God is good despite our bad situations and circumstances.

When our lives are examined by future generations, this message must be clear: Our praise and worship was not restricted to favorable circumstances. We were a people with a big God who cast His marvelous, enormous shadow over our moment in history—and we loved Him and praised Him for who He is.

The prophet Habakkuk put it best. This affirmation is particularly meaningful because he had been challenging God, asking Him, in effect, why bad things happen. Here is what he concluded:

Though the fig tree should not blossom, and there be no fruit on the vines, though the yield of the olive should fail, and the fields produce no food, though the flock should be cut off from the fold, and there be no cattle in the stalls, yet I will exult in the Lord, I will rejoice in the God of my salvation. The Lord God is my strength, and He has made my feet like hinds' feet, and makes me walk on my high places. —Habakkuk 3:17–19

Let us pray that others will clearly see that our trail is marked by footprints that show God as our refuge, a life that is a resource to others, a spirit of remembrance for what matters most, and a soul that praises God in all things.

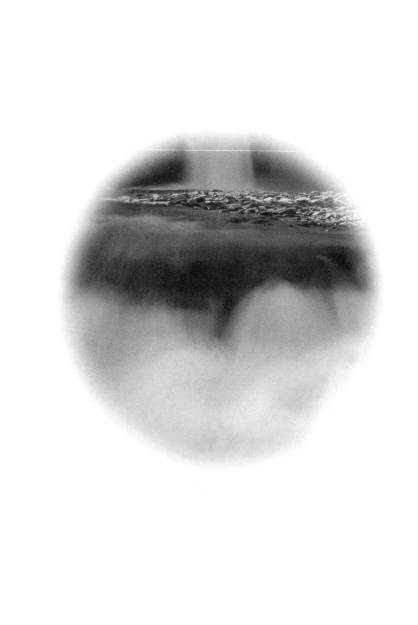

Live
the
Truth

Remember when comedian Bill Cosby called on entertainers to get rid of their foul, filthy language so they would be better examples to the African-American community and to our young people? You would have thought he asked people to commit suicide. He was called a few not-so-nice names and told that no one needed his "moralizing."

I admire Cosby and his courage. He was willing to speak up for something that seems to be going out of style today—a sense of responsibility to set an example for those who look up to us. You'd have to be blind to overlook the way that today's celebrities influence the behavior of young people. And in an age when many traditional families are falling apart, it is increasingly important that children have strong role models to look up to.

For many years, I have spoken to different professional sports teams. I have met and known quite a few athletes who live exemplary lives and are committed Christians. They are shining lights, and they take their responsibility as role models very seriously. They use their recognition and platform to influence others, especially their young, admiring fans.

It is regrettable that the media doesn't pay more attention to these fine men and women. Over the last ten years or so, a growing number of other professional athletes (and public figures) have rejected the notion that with their visibility comes the responsibility to be role models. In fact, the "bad boy" image is worn as a badge of honor. Indiscretions and brushes with the law are considered a necessary part of their resume.

These individuals feel no shame or embarrassment. They shrug off their bad behavior and poor choices as if to say, "There's more to come." The message to young, aspiring athletes is that you can live and act just about any way you want to and still be successful. The same goes for many other people in the limelight today, like entertainers, businesspeople, politicians.

And this doesn't apply just to celebrities. When I was growing up, the adults in our city had a greater awareness and appreciation for their responsibility to set and project a good example. For example, there was a no-profanity rule in our neighborhood barbershop. If one of the customers would slip, someone would say, "Hey, watch your mouth. There are kids in here." I remember when a man was kicked out of the barbershop because he just kept using foul language.

No matter who you are—a dad or mom, a pastor, a student, an executive, or an employee—chances are that somebody is watching you. Their eyes are on you. You are influencing them. So you need to decide who you want to be, and what you want to project to others.

I was reminded recently of the profound power of modeling when Karen and I visited our eldest son, Bryan, and his family. Just before we left the house on a Sunday evening to attend church, our grandson Quentin, age three, said to our son,

"Daddy, I want to bring my Bible to church." His mother went and got his "Bible" (actually a children's devotional book) and gave it to him.

Then Quentin looked at his dad and saw that he had his Bible tucked under his right arm. So Quentin tucked his "Bible" under his right arm. As I witnessed that scene I smiled and thought to myself, *He wants to be just like his dad.*

IN AND THROUGH US

Living as authentic Christians means that as followers of Christ we not only embrace the truth of God's Word intellectually, but we also embrace it incarnationally, surrendering to the Living Word, Jesus Christ. He lives His life in and through us, empowering us to live out the truth of His Son before the world. We carry with us a sober but joyful responsibility to represent Him and to influence others for Him because we are aware that there are eyes on us.

Further, Jesus Christ has changed our destiny and declared us to be citizens of heaven while we live on earth. The certainty of our eternal destiny dictates how we should live and underscores a sacred obligation to reflect the values of heaven through how we live down here. Our responsibility to be light to the world is especially critical in a culture where the erosion of moral spiritual absolutes has left us a legacy of uncertainty. Behavior is increasingly unrestrained. I am reminded of the book of Judges in the Old Testament where it said, "Everyone did what was right in his own eyes" (Judges 21:25).

We have bought into the lie that all that matters is here and now. If it feels good to me, then it is right for me. Morality and character are fluid—defined by the opinion shapers and the image power brokers, according to their own desires rather than by what is true and what is right. This is Paul's point in Philippians 3:17–21:

Brethren, join in following my example, and observe those who walk according to the pattern you have in us. For many walk, of whom I often told you, and now tell you even weeping, that they are enemies of the cross of Christ, whose end is destruction, whose god is their appetite, and whose glory is in their shame, who set their minds on earthly things. For our citizenship is in heaven, from which also we eagerly wait for a Savior, the Lord Jesus Christ; who will transform the body of our humble state into conformity with the body of His glory, by the exertion of the power that He has even to subject all things to Himself.

In verse 17 he invites the Philippian Christians to follow his example and to pattern their lives after those who exemplify the same godly character qualities that Paul is committed to demonstrating. Paul is not saying that he is perfect, but he wants others to know that he is very much aware that he has a responsibility and obligation to walk according to the truth.

He understands the power of example—truth lived and demonstrated and not just spoken. His message is, "Catch what we believe by watching how we live."

Our youngest son, Bryndan, is a youth pastor. His mentor, the senior pastor, is a wonderful, godly man. In a phone conversation Bryndan said to me, "Dad, I am learning so much about ministry and the spiritual life by hanging out with the pastor and *watching how he responds to people and situations.*" This is putting flesh around theology—the pastor is giving Bryndan a compelling motivation to live the same type of life.

Paul describes in scathing terms the "enemies of the cross" whose lives are not worth emulating. There are some so-called believers whose lifestyles do not glorify Christ, and they are bringing others down with them. It is not only appropriate but also our responsibility to point out these people and to warn others to avoid being drawn into the wake of their negative, destructive example and influence.

Both of our sons are in the ministry, and I have on occasion warned them to stay away from certain individuals who I knew were up to no good. In fact, I remember once pointing out a man to one of my sons and saying, "You see that man over there? I suggest you stay away from him because he is a fool, and his foolishness will bring him down."

Next, Paul exhorts us to remember that we are people of destiny, citizens of heaven (vs. 20). And each time we choose what this world values over the surpassing treasure of the eternal kingdom, we deny our heavenly citizenship.

How we live tells the truth about what we really believe.

I am a citizen of the United States of America, and I have a passport. For most of the countries I have visited through the years, I needed to secure a visa, which is permission to enter that country and to stay for a period of time. This visa says that I am just visiting, but I also hold on to my passport because I am not going to renounce my citizenship. My passport reminds me that my home is in the United States of America, and I am eventually going to return to where I belong.

In the same way, as Christians we do not belong to this world. We are here on a "work visa." God has left us here to accomplish a task and to get the job done by both word and example. We work and live like citizens of heaven (v. 20). This is our high noble calling and our destiny. We "eagerly wait" to see our Savior. And one day He will transform these broken down, decaying bodies into glorious, eternal bodies suited for our heavenly home (v. 21).

Why does Paul emphasize our heavenly citizenship? Because it is our motivation for living a life worth following. In short, we need to live now like we belong to heaven. When others examine our lives, they will want to be like us and, more importantly, like Christ.

An Open Book

As a citizen of heaven who realizes that eyes are on you, I want to encourage you to prayerfully ask God to make the four important perspectives from the pen of the apostle Paul a conscious part of your Christian walk. First, *live your life well, remembering that others are watching you.* Second Corinthians 3:2–3 says, "You are our letter, written in our hearts, known and read by all men; being manifested that you are a letter of Christ, cared for by us, written not with ink, but with the Spirit of the living God, not on tablets of stone, but on tablets of human hearts." Paul is saying to the church of Corinth, "I have watched you. I have seen how you live. I don't need a letter about you, because you are the letter about yourself."

Once again, how we live tells the truth about what we really believe. Others are reading our lives. Through the years, I have had friends who are applying for a job or another position list me as a reference on their application. It's always a joy to me to be able to write a few words, confidently endorsing and commending someone that I know. It's a thrill to be able to say that I have known this person for a number of years and have seen the demonstration of Christlike character and integrity in and through this person's life.

We are writing an open letter by how we live. What kind of letter is your life writing? When people read your life, what will they learn about you? What will they discover? Will they see a life of consistency, one who is living like a citizen of heaven or will they conclude, "This person sure knows a lot of the Bible, but they don't seem to live by the Bible they know."

Jonathan Edwards has been called America's greatest theologian. He was a scholar of immense intellectual capacity, and he wrote voluminously. He was a pastor, a revivalist/evangelist, a missionary to Indians, and a college president. He also was a devoted husband and the father of eleven children. It can be argued that Edward's greatest legacy was his passionate commitment to be a godly example of what he believed, wrote about, and preached to others. He understood that his life was really the theology that others would read. Is it any wonder that so many of his descendants walked with God and made an incredible impact for the cause of Christ during their moments in history?

BE THE TRUTH

This leads to the second perspective: *Be the truth you want others to know and believe.* Take a look at what Paul said as a mentor to his young disciple Timothy: "Let no one look down on your youthfulness, but rather in speech, conduct, love, faith and purity, show yourself an example of those who believe" (I Timothy 4:12).

I prefer an alternate translation of the last line in the verse. Instead of "an example *of* those who believe" it could have been translated "an example *to* those who believe." The message here is that Timothy's effectiveness as a pastor and leader is not ultimately determined by his grasp of theology and the sharpening of his pastoral skills.

Dr. Howard Hendricks, a professor at Dallas Theological Seminary for more than fifty years, says that one of the things he has learned in all these years is to be unimpressed with how much of Scripture a person knows. I've heard him say more than once, "The Bible was not given to satisfy our curiosity but to transform our lives." Of course every follower of Christ needs to be a disciplined, serious student of the Word of God, but for what reason? So that our *lives* will be conformed to the image of the living truth, Jesus Christ.

I know a young pastor who was "mentored" by an older man who was a very prominent, successful pastor with a national reputation. Unfortunately, this older man led a sordid life. He was immoral and dishonest, but he had a dominating, powerful personality and, as the saying goes, he could preach the birds out of the trees. He was accountable to no one, but because of his enormously persuasive public gifts and abilities, people rationalized and pushed aside the evidence of his glaring inconsistencies and wrongdoings.

This young pastor confided in me that he didn't want to be like the man who mentored him. But the story does not have a good ending. Some of the same traits and character flaws he saw in his mentor have been absorbed in his life, and he is becoming like what he saw.

The integrity of our Christianity depends on our ability to be examples, models of what we believe. If people disagree with us and don't like us, don't let it be because we are hypocrites. Don't preach a biblical message and then make flimsy excuses for not living what you have told others to do. You know the tired old line, "Don't do as I do, just do as I say."

We need to be committed to the sincere struggle of every moment of our lives applying the truth of God's Word. In this way others cannot escape the truth we proclaim. They are drawn to a model of legitimate, authentic Christianity.

INTENTIONALLY IMPRINT

Third, *intentionally pass on to others what you have learned.* In Philippians 4:9, Paul tells the church at Philippi, "The things you have learned and received and heard and seen in me, practice these things." Then in 2 Timothy 2:2 he advises Timothy, "The things which you have heard from me in the presence of many witnesses, these entrust to faithful men, who will be able to teach others also."

Paul intentionally imprinted the lives of the Christians at Philippi, and he tells Timothy, "Just as I have intentionally imprinted your life, do the same for others so that they will do the same as well." We should also seek out others to intentionally imprint their lives with lessons we have learned along the journey. We need to share out of the richness of our successes and the valleys of our failures.

The Bible calls this discipleship. I don't know where I would be had it not been for the godly men and women who have influenced my life. They invested in me, and I saw in them what I could become. They loved me and marked my life and shared lessons, advice, and council that has protected me from bad choices and disaster. People like my dad, Burton Cathie, Douglas MacCorkle, Robertson McQuilkin, Walford Thompson, Bill Bright, and others. These men came alongside me at strategic points of my development and were used by God to encourage me and sometimes to correct and challenge me.

Their example has encouraged me to do the same for others. I am committed to imprinting my life on the lives of others. As we establish mentoring and discipleship relationships, the truth of God's Word is seen in flesh and blood. We become tangible expressions of God's love and a source of encouragement.

Several years ago I started something that has become one of the most significant things I have ever done in my life and ministry. It has brought me inexpressible joy. I asked ten friends who are Christian leaders to join me in mentoring younger potential leaders. After identifying the candidates, we each "adopted" four of these young men. We have given them access to our lives and have made a commitment to do all we can to help them grow as men of God. After all, someone did this for us, and now it's our turn to do it for someone else.

SUCCESS CAN BE DEFINED AS THE VALUE WE ADD AND ACCRUE TO OURSELVES, BUT SIGNIFICANCE IS GIVING VALUE TO OTHERS.

What's really exciting to me is that these young men have caught the vision and are mentoring others as well. All of us know people who are open and teachable. We need to come alongside them, put an arm on their shoulder and say, "I want you to know that I am praying for you. If there is anything that I can do to be of help or encouragement to you, just let me know. In fact I would love to get together with you on a regular basis for a time of prayer and sharing." Place in their hands a book, a tape, or CD of a message that will bless and encourage them. Periodically call them and let them know that you are thinking about them and praying for them. Be available to them.

If we are going to intentionally invest in others, we are forced to make a decision. We have to decide if we want to pursue success or significance. Success can be defined as the value we add and accrue to ourselves, but significance is giving value to others. As citizens of heaven we are called to pursue significance. How are you valuing others?

SERVE SACRIFICIALLY

And that's the fourth perspective. We are called to live a life of sacrifice for the glory of God and for the sake of others. In 2 Timothy 4:6, Paul makes an interesting statement. He is facing imminent execution for the cause of Christ. I guess you could say he is preaching his own eulogy to his disciple Timothy. He says, "For I am already being poured out as a drink offering, and the time of my departure has come."

Did you catch that expression, "being poured out as a drink offering"? He said the same thing in Philippians 2:17, with a little more explanation: "But even if I am being poured out as a drink offering upon *the sacrifice and service of your faith*, I rejoice and share my joy with you all." He is saying that his entire life is a thanksgiving sacrifice for the growth and development of others.

No doubt Paul had in mind the drink offering referenced by David in I Chronicles 11:17–19. It had been years since David drank from the cool refreshing well in Bethlehem. He verbalized his craving: "Oh that someone would give me water to drink from the well of Bethlehem, which is by the gate!" (v. 17). Three of his mighty men heard what he said, but there was a problem. Bethlehem was under the control of their enemy, the Philistines. But these three men loved their leader and wanted to do something to show their appreciation and gratitude for what David meant to them. So they risked their lives, entered enemy territory, and filled the goat skins with that liquid treasure.

I can see the scene now: "David, do you remember that well in Bethlehem? Well, look what we have for you." David was so overcome by this incredible act of sacrifice and service that he considered it profane to drink what he had craved. He turned the moment into an act of worship. He symbolically poured the water on the ground (v. 18) because he was even more grateful and thankful to God for the sacrificial service of his men. That's why he said in verse 19, "Be it far from me before my God that I should do this. Shall I drink the blood of these men who went at the risk of their lives? For at the risk of their lives they bought it."

We are not called to a comfortable, cultural Christianity. We are citizens of heaven who live out the values and perspectives of our heavenly kingdom in the context of this fallen world. We, too, should be "drink offerings." Just as Paul and David did not want to do anything that would impede the spiritual growth and development of those who were looking to them as examples, we need to take our eyes off of what we want and focus on what *others* need. Our lifestyles need to reflect this love and commitment to others.

At this point, I realize that my editors would love for me to give a few illustrations or examples to put some handles on what I've just said, and I'm tempted to do so. But I am not going to do that. Sometimes we just need to wrestle with the implications and applications of certain truths with regards to the context in which we live.

Our relationship with Christ is not a private affair. It is a public declaration to others concerning the legitimacy of the gospel, and it is a statement concerning our country of origin. We are citizens of heaven who should be aware that others are watching us. It is not a question of whether we want to be a model. We are, like it or not.

What are we doing about it?

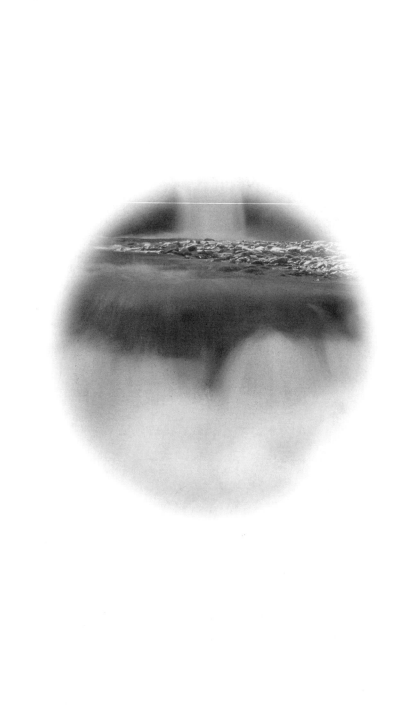

Get
Ready

You're sitting at home enjoying a quiet Friday evening with your family. The past month has been extremely busy, but this was the last day of school, and now the kids are out for the summer. Everyone is relieved that the pressure is off, and they're excited about the weeks of vacation coming up.

You clear the table and put the dishes into the dishwasher. The family is gathered in the family room to watch a movie together. You put a disk into the DVD player, you kick back with a bowl of popcorn and a soft drink, and you put your mind into neutral. All cares and concerns have been suspended for the moment. You're enjoying your family and one of your favorite movies.

Then the phone rings. You answer it, and you hear a woman saying, "This is the White House calling, and an assistant to the president would like to speak to you."

Your first thought is that this is surely a joke, and so you say, "Okay, who is this really, and who do you want to talk to?" But the woman responds, "No, I assure you, this is not a joke. I am connecting you to the president's assistant." And almost immediately you hear a voice of a man who calls you by name and confirms that this indeed is the White House calling, and he is a special assistant to the president of the United States.

You leap to your feet, forgetting that a bowl of popcorn is sitting in your lap, and popcorn flies everywhere. You fumble to find the remote to mute the sound on the TV. The kids protest loudly, and you shush them and mouth the words, "Be quiet, this is the White House!" Everyone, including your wife, rolls their eyes and says, "Yeah, right."

You quickly go to another room. You say to the man on the line, "You must have the wrong person. Why are you calling me? Have I done something wrong?" The president's assistant responds with an obvious smile in his voice, "Oh no, you haven't done anything wrong at all. I'm calling because the President and the First Lady will be visiting your city next Friday, and they thought it would be a great idea to visit a family in the community. Your family was selected, and we checked you out, and we think your family is a great choice. The President and First Lady would like to visit your home and have dinner with your family."

You are overwhelmed and your mind turns into mush . . . you don't know what to say. Questions and thoughts are filling your mind. A voice brings you back to the present: "Are you still there?"

You reply, "Oh yes, sorry . . . when do I have to give you an answer?"

"In an hour. Talk it over with your wife and call me back." You jot down the number and hang up. You collapse in a chair, your jaw drops, and you say out loud, "I can't believe what I just heard."

By now your wife walks into the room. You tell her about the conversation and the decision you need to make. At first she covers her mouth in shocked disbelief. Then it settles in. You both conclude that, although your lives will be disrupted over the next week, this is an opportunity of a lifetime. Both of you return to the family room and tell the kids. They are ecstatic. So you call the president's assistant and you say you've agreed to host the president of the United States for dinner.

For the next week the entire family is focused on one thing—preparing for the First Couple's visit. The thought that the most powerful man in the free world will be sitting at your dining room table is almost too much to handle. Although the White House says, "Please don't go out of your way" in preparing for the visit, you know you need to put your best foot forward. This is one time that the whole family is in agreement. Everything has to be just right. You have to make a good impression. Chances are you will never entertain another president and his wife.

The lawn is cut and manicured. The hedges are trimmed. You rent a pressure sprayer to wash the driveway, clean the house from top to bottom, and repaint the laundry room. You hire professionals to clean the carpet, and decide this might be just the time to replace that tattered old sofa in the living room.

The big day finally arrives. The good silverware is polished, and the china that is only used on special occasions is sparkling clean. Your wife learns what food the president likes and is preparing his favorite meal. You've even given special attention to what everyone is going to wear. You are ready, but you still have a lump in your throat as a small fleet of vehicles arrives on your street. . . .

"HE'S COMING!"

It's amazing how quickly our priorities become focused when someone you consider important comes to visit. Though you will likely never host the president of the United States, perhaps you've had your boss, or your pastor, over for dinner. Perhaps you've worked until the wee hours of the morning cleaning your home so you can host your in-laws for a holiday gathering, and there's no way your mother-in-law is going to find dirt on your shelves!

But sometime (and it may be soon) you will be in the presence of someone far greater than the president of the United States. Eternity in heaven means literally entering the physical presence of Jesus Christ. And just as you would pour yourself into preparing for the president's visit, we should even more dedicate ourselves to preparing to meet the Savior face-to-face.

The intentional pursuit of holiness is the ultimate act of grateful worship to our Lord.

First John 3:2–3 tells us, "Beloved, now we are children of God, and it has not appeared as yet what we shall be. We know that, when He appears, we shall be like Him, because we shall see Him just as He is. And everyone who has this hope fixed on Him *purifies himself, just as He is pure.*"

In one sense, this passage is a warning. Jesus is coming without advanced notice. He could arrive before you finish reading this chapter. Like company that shows up unannounced and sees your house in less than presentable shape, many people will be embarrassed when our Lord returns. They are not prepared.

I remember when I was twelve and was smoking cigarettes

with some of my friends. Suddenly someone told me, "Your mom is coming!"

I was petrified because I didn't want her to see what I was doing. So I hid between two buildings until she walked by. I was her child, but I wasn't living up to what she had taught me and was ashamed to let her see. In the same way, Jesus is coming unannounced, but there will be no informant warning us, and we won't be able to hide.

WHILE WE WAIT

So while we wait, what do we do? When He does come back, John tells us, "we shall be like Him" (I John 3:2).

This is an amazing statement. When I am in His presence, I shall be holy, just as He is holy. I won't even have the *capacity* for rebellion or pride or disobedience. It's hard to imagine no longer struggling with the jealousy, envy, anger, lust, materialism, greed, dishonesty, and so much more that is a natural part of my fleshly existence. All that will be gone, done away with, over. Instant, glorious, permanent removal. I will look upon the pure, holy Savior with pure, holy eyes.

But in the meantime, we can't throw up our hands and say, "What's the use? We can't help sinning, so it's a good thing we're forgiven. We'll do our best to keep our sin under wraps and do a little damage control so that it doesn't get completely out of hand." John says the fact that we have an unannounced appointment with the perfect, pure Lamb of God who has borne our sins should lead us to give ourselves relentlessly to the removal of sin in our lives. The intentional pursuit of holiness is the ultimate act of grateful worship to our Lord for delivering us from the kingdom of darkness and securing our eternal destiny (Romans 12:1).

To be members of the family of God means that we are living in constant preparation for our ultimate destination— the very presence of God. That's why John says in I John 3:3, "Everyone who has this hope fixed on Him purifies himself, just as He is pure." The word *hope* is defined by the context. This hope is not anticipation based on uncertain speculation, but the confident assurance that we indeed are going to see Him, be with Him, and be like Him (pure) one day.

Holiness is our calling. God's promises are our confidence. I don't know about you, but this confidence causes me to bow and worship before the lover of my soul. How I want to see Him and have His purity. But He has not yet appeared. We're waiting. So what do we do while we wait? The answer is, we are to purify ourselves, just as He is pure.

Some years back, while I was speaking in another country, Karen and our eldest son, Bryan, who was two at the time, were staying with my parents. On the day I returned, they arrived at the airport only to find out the plane had been delayed.

From what they tell me, Bryan was not having a very good day at all. He was fidgety and generally not cooperating. He had to be disciplined several times. Karen says the only thing that seemed to help for a while was saying, "Daddy is coming very soon." Bryan would straighten up for a while and be on his best behavior.

Just as my wife's words, "Daddy is coming," to a distracted two-year-old restrained his behavior, so also a motivation for pursuing purity is found in our accountability to our Lord and living in anticipation of His coming. We long to be with Him and like Him.

We must never become blinded to sin's effect in our lives. About ten years ago I started wearing eyeglasses. I'll never forget the first time I put those glasses on. The world suddenly came into focus, and I was amazed at how I hadn't realized how dull my vision had become. I had grown accustomed to something less than 20/20 vision. In the same way, sin deceives us into thinking that we're all right, that everything is okay. But we're headed toward certain blindness. And the more we compromise with sin, the duller our vision becomes. Our hearts become callous, and holiness is reduced to something we may talk about, though it becomes increasingly removed from the core of our Christian experience.

Sin puts the brakes on God's work in our lives. I have known of many people who were living in unrepentant sin. And God still blessed their ministry in the sense that He has honored His Word and the prayers of others. But every person I have talked to who went through a time of unrepentant sin has confessed that they were miserable and that they paid a price.

It is impossible to serve two masters. The Holy Spirit living within us convicts us of sin and empowers us to overcome it. But when we resist His promptings by refusing to repent, we're asking for misery and to be disciplined by God.

No, I do not believe in sinless perfection in this life. When we see Him, then we will be perfect without sin. But as I said earlier, this does not mean that we should accommodate and make excuses for the sins we commit during our sojourn on earth. We are called to run from sin and to pursue holiness. As soon as we realize we commit a sin, we should instantly confess it and turn away from it. Sin is not neutral; it is destructive. It's kind of like that old television commercial where an auto mechanic tells us that in the long run it is cheaper to spend a relatively small amount of money on regular maintenance than it is to neglect our car. Sooner or later, we're going to have a very costly problem. He says, "You either pay me now, or pay me later."

THE ULTIMATE ACT OF HUMILITY

Sin always has a price tag. But what should we do when we sin? How should we handle it? In a word, *repent.*

There are two parts to repentance. First, we are to acknowledge that we have sinned, and then we are to turn from the sin. Look closely at I John 1:7–9:

> *If we walk in the light as He Himself is in the light, we have fellowship with one another, and the blood of Jesus His Son cleanses us from all sin. If we say that we have no sin, we are deceiving ourselves, and the truth is not in us. If we confess our sins, He is faithful and righteous to forgive us our sins and to cleanse us from all unrighteousness.*

Both verses give us an excellent descriptive definition of biblical repentance. Repentance is both a point—a specific act—and a process. And it is important to understand that although verse 7 comes before verse 9, "confession" (v. 9) of sin takes place *before* we can "walk in the light."

Confession of sin is a very specific act. The word *confess* comes from the Greek word *homologeo,* which literally means to "say the same thing." When we confess our sins, we are not only acknowledging that we have done something wrong, we are *agreeing* with God's assessment of what we have done. In other words, we come completely clean about what we have done. We don't make excuses or minimize our sin in any way, and we don't reluctantly acknowledge that we have done something wrong.

Confession has to do with sincere heart agreement and not

just the words we say. Since we want His holiness to be our experience, we ask Him to change us to do what is right in the future.

IMPERFECT, UNHOLY, AND WRONG

Through the years I've run into quite a few people who said they were sorry about what they had done. But I sensed that they were more sorry and embarrassed that they got caught. They were really more concerned about how they appeared to other people, and so in order to get off the "hot seat," they gave verbal acknowledgment and even said the right words. But their confession lacked sincerity.

God knows the condition of our hearts, and He desires complete, transparent truth. And confession of sin is the ultimate act of humility. When we specifically confess our sin, we're saying we are imperfect, unholy, and wrong. We declare that God is utterly perfect, unspeakably holy, and never wrong. It is this acknowledgment—our total, unreserved agreement with God's assessment—that releases the flood of forgiveness and cleansing.

Some time ago, I spoke at a conference and ran into a friend I hadn't seen in more than fifteen years. It was so good to see George again (not his real name). We sat down over coffee and got caught up. He brought me up to date on his family and his work. I shared with him what was going on with our family and some of the highlights in my ministry.

Then there was a bit of an awkward pause in the conversation. I sensed that George wanted to tell me something, but for whatever reason, he couldn't get it out. Not wanting to pry, I thought perhaps the best thing to do was to relieve the tension by saying, "Why don't we finish this a little later? I'm going to go back to my room and look over my message for this evening."

But as I got up to leave, George said, "Crawford, do you have a few more minutes? There's more to my story that I want to share with you." He told me that about eight years earlier he hit the wall spiritually. He was working long hours and neglecting his relationship with his wife, and they began to drift apart. Although he was regularly attending church and even involved in a small group, his personal time of worship and reading the Bible was sporadic and inconsistent. He felt tired and gripped by a sense of loneliness.

He began feeling a growing attraction to a woman at work. One day their eyes connected, and it ignited something in both of them. They began to flirt with each other and find excuses to spend more time together. It wasn't long before they were involved in an affair that lasted for several months.

George described it as the darkest, most miserable time in his life. The guilt almost caused him to lose his mind. But the Holy Spirit was working on him. Driving home one evening after a rendezvous with the other woman, he began to weep and found himself pleading with God for forgiveness.

When he walked in the house that evening he knew what he had to do. Telling his wife the truth was the hardest thing he had ever done in his life. They talked for hours, and he saw the agony and deep betrayal of trust he caused his wife. She almost left him. But she didn't.

He broke off the relationship with the other woman and took ownership for his sin. He and his wife went to their pastor, and he confessed what he had done. They both went through counseling to help strengthen their marriage, and George submitted himself to the spiritual care and restoration of three godly men.

As I sat across the table and looked at George's face, I saw the freedom and joy of repentance written across his face. It was clear that this man had turned to God for forgiveness and restoration.

WALK TOWARD CHRIST

But acknowledging and submitting fully to what God says about our sin—and thereby experiencing His forgiveness and cleansing—is not complete repentance. This is a reason why many of us keep slipping back into old sinful habits. We *have* sincerely confessed our sins. We *have* experienced His cleansing and forgiveness. The problem is we have not embraced new patterns of holiness that keep us moving toward the heart of the Savior and away from sin.

To be sure, as long as we are on this side of heaven, we will always be tempted, and we will often sin. But the more we intentionally and authentically pursue Christlikeness, sin will lose its control and dominance in our lives (Romans 6:19). This second part of repentance is what John is referring to in 1 John 1:7 when he says, "but if we walk in the light . . . the blood of Jesus His Son cleanses from all sin." Once we confess our sin, God wants us to walk away from the sin.

Where do we go? We walk *toward* Christ. We make a decision to intentionally pursue holiness and "walk in the light." The word *walk* suggests new patterns of behavior that express the light and righteousness of our Savior. It is the determination to do whatever is necessary to distance ourselves from the sin and therefore bring ourselves closer to His light and His holiness.

It may mean public confession, submitting to an accountability group, strengthening our spiritual disciplines, or seeking godly biblical counsel. Whatever it takes to break the cycle or control of sin in our lives, we must be willing and committed to do it. There is too much at stake. There's joy, peace, power, love, direction, and indescribable communion with God when we walk in the light. Let me encourage you to step out of the shadows into His holiness. Sin is a deceiver that pushes us deeper into darkness. Confess your sin, and then do what it takes to overcome it.

CONFESSION OF SIN GETS US BACK ON THE ROAD TOWARD HOLINESS, BUT WALKING IN THE LIGHT GIVES US SPIRITUAL MOMENTUM.

I grew up in the Northeast, where we were used to driving in snowy, icy conditions. We now live in Atlanta, where we may get two or three inches of snow a year. Karen and I have learned that when it does snow, the better part of wisdom is to stay off the roads. Drivers in Atlanta are not used to driving in winter conditions, and as a result there are accidents galore.

One common mistake inexperienced drivers make is to slow down before driving up an icy hill. I once saw a driver slow down and lose all his momentum, and it was not long before he lost all traction and slid right into a parked car.

Confession of sin gets us back on the road toward holiness, but walking in the light gives us spiritual momentum. Don't stop moving forward—you will have a spiritual accident.

We should be motivated to pursue holiness because the King is coming. Oh, what a day that will be! But until then, we have stuff we need to clean up and get in order. And we need to take care of it now. In fact, we need to live ready for the ultimate appointment.

For a fuller treatment on sin and repentance, let me suggest that you read my book *Make It Home Before Dark.*

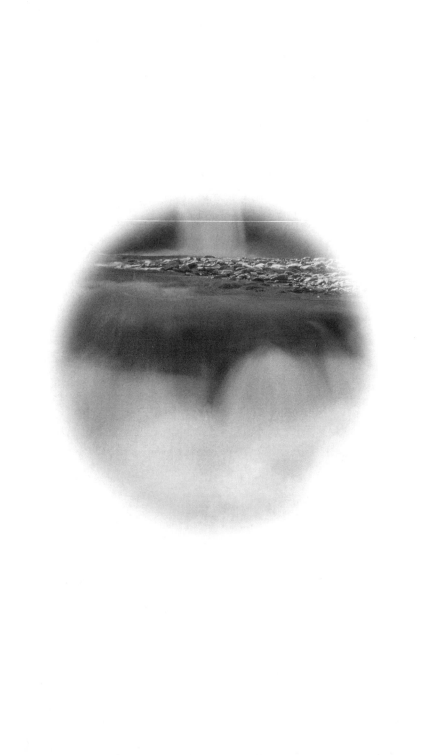

Hold On!

In my briefcase is a letter from my oldest sister, Elaina. As I've already mentioned, she died of breast cancer. I found it in her apartment after the funeral, never mailed. She wrote it during a time of great discomfort and suffering; she was going through chemotherapy, she had lost over seventy pounds, and all her hair had fallen out. Let me share a few excerpts from the letter with you:

> C. W., I have not stopped giving thanks for you, remembering you in my prayers. I want you to know that I appreciate all you have done for me. Please continue to pray for me. God continues to bless me. Each day I feel stronger in my faith, although my body is weak. There are many people helping me and taking care of me. My church and my pastor have been wonderful, and my friends have lined up to aid me in whatever I need. The road has been a trying one. But there has been SOMEONE there to weather the storm with me. There are so many blessings being given to me since I have been sick. The Lord has showered me

with His favor. There is always something or someone who keeps my spirit up and encourages me to hold on.

When I'm going through a hard time, I read the letter, and God whispers to me, "Don't lose heart. Keep moving." God wonderfully and compassionately met my sister at a point of need, touching Elaina through the arms of her church and her friends. She also knew that, in her darkest moments, God was there to "weather the storm" with her. So she didn't faint in her soul.

I've had my share of dark stretches in life. I've found myself in circumstances and situations that required far more than I had to give. I have been blindsided by a phone call from my sister telling me, "Mom just had a major heart attack, and it doesn't look like she's going to make it." Or the call that informed me that my wife and youngest daughter had been in a very serious car accident.

I remember when our ministry faced an unexpected, major financial challenge . . . when I was misunderstood and even betrayed by someone I loved and trusted . . . when I felt the agony of having to confront someone I loved dearly about sin, only to be personally attacked and labeled a "legalist." Like you, I have experienced those times when I sensed God's presence was veiled at a time when I needed His direction; or seasons of intense temptation in which I felt as if I were hanging on by a thread; or times of general pressure in which deadlines and unanticipated surprises pushed me under the surface and it seemed as if I was going to drown; or . . . or . . . or . . .

I know you've been there too. Sometimes we are so overwhelmed that we lose perspective and cave in to the pressures and challenges of this life, this journey. We say, "What's the use?" We lose our intensity in following Christ. Reversals, disappointments, and unfulfilled expectations can tarnish our vision and drive us into cynicism.

But that's not an option for the citizen of heaven. Jesus never promised any of His followers an easy time. In fact, He says just the opposite. In John 16:33, for example, Jesus says, "These things I have spoken to you, that in Me you may have peace. In the world you have tribulation, but take courage; I have overcome the world." Or take Matthew 5:10–12: "Blessed are those who have been persecuted for the sake of righteousness, for theirs is the kingdom of heaven. Blessed are you when men cast insults at you, and persecute you, and say all kinds of evil against you falsely, on account of Me. Rejoice, and be glad, for your reward in heaven is great, for so they persecuted the prophets who were before you."

My sister's experience makes me think of 2 Corinthians 4:16: "Our outer man is decaying, yet our inner man is being renewed day by day." We are born to die. Every living thing will die. You can exercise, eat right, and take vitamins, but you will still die.

*W*HAT HAPPENS IN US SHOULD NOT BE DETERMINED BY WHAT HAPPENS TO US.

The older we grow, the more we are reminded that our bodies are, indeed, decaying. Although we are breathing and have a heartbeat, the decaying process has begun. And there is nothing we can do about it. You can clip your body, wig it, suction it, lift it, augment it—and in the end it doesn't matter. Your body will break down.

But we can do something about the development and vitality of our souls. The message of 2 Corinthians 4 is clear: What happens *in* us should not be determined by what happens *to* us. In fact, what happens to us should make our souls stronger, more resolute, more committed to our Savior. My sister captured this spirit when she wrote in her letter, "Every day I feel stronger in my faith, although my body is weak." Allow the circumstances of life to drive you to the heart of the Savior.

NOT *IF*, BUT *HOW*

You've probably read Scriptures that make it clear that suffering and hard times play an irrevocable, intrinsic part in our growth and development as followers of Christ. But right now, take a few moments to consider afresh these passages in light of *your* life over the years:

> *For to you it has been granted for Christ's sake, not only to believe in Him, but also to suffer for His sake.* —Philippians 1:29

> *Consider it all joy, my brethren, when you encounter various trials, knowing that the testing of your faith produces endurance. And let endurance have its perfect result, that you may be perfect and complete, lacking in nothing.* —James 1:2–4

> *In this you greatly rejoice, even though now for a little while, if necessary, you have been distressed by various trials, that the proof of your faith, being more precious than gold which is perishable, even though tested by fire, may be found to result in praise and glory and honor at the revelation of Jesus Christ; and though you have not seen Him, you love Him, and though you do not see Him now, but believe in Him, you greatly rejoice with joy inexpressible and full of glory, obtaining as the outcome of your faith the salvation of your souls.* —1 Peter 1:6–9

> *For what credit is there if, when you sin and are harshly treated, you endure it with patience? But if when you do what is right and suffer for it you patiently endure it, this finds favor with God.* —1 Peter 2:20

Who shall separate us from the love of Christ? Shall tribulation, or distress, or persecution, or famine, or nakedness, or peril, or sword? Just as it is written, "For Thy sake we are being put to death all day long; we were considered as sheep to be slaughtered."

But in all these things we overwhelmingly conquer through Him who loved us. For I am convinced that neither death, nor life, nor angels, nor principalities, nor things present, nor things to come, nor powers, nor height, nor depth, nor any other created thing, shall be able to separate us from the love of God, which is in Christ Jesus our Lord.   —Romans 8:35–39

Scriptures like these make it clear that the question we must face is not *if* we will suffer, but *how* we will keep moving when we are visited with hard times. How do we endure?

We live our lives under the sovereign hand of God. We don't control what happens to us. We can only *respond* to what happens. And if you think about it, we have only two choices on how to respond to the inevitable suffering we will face in this life: We can endure it, or we can give up. And that really leaves us with one choice, because to the follower of Christ—a citizen of heaven—giving up is not an option. We must endure.

THREE DECISIONS

I want to suggest that there are three crucial decisions that, as citizens of heaven, we must make when we are visited by hard times. First, *we must choose not to lose heart.* Look closely at 2 Corinthians 4:16–18:

Therefore, we do not lose heart, but though our outer man is decaying, yet our inner man is being renewed day by day. For momentary, light affliction is producing for us an eternal weight of glory far beyond all comparison, while we look not at the things which are seen, but at the things which are not seen;

for the things which are seen are temporal, but the things which are not seen are eternal.

To "lose heart" means to faint in our souls. It means to be passionless, dried up, and beaten up in the very core of our being. But Paul's words scream at us, "Don't quit. Don't give up. Tell your heart to keep beating, keep pursuing. It's worth it!" The point is, no matter what happens, we don't cave in to our circumstances. We don't allow ourselves to be so overcome by discouragement that we are washed away by despondency and despair.

But verse 17 puts it all in perspective. Paul says what all we go through in this life is "momentary" and "light." Further, it is producing in us an "*eternal* weight of glory far beyond all comparison." Even if we have experienced a lifetime of hardship and suffering, those years are nothing when seen in light of eternity.

God takes note of our suffering and pain. Look at these sweet words in Psalm 56:8 NASB: "You have taken account of my wanderings; put my tears in Your bottle. Are they not in Your book?" And Psalm 126:5–6: "Those who sow in tears shall reap with joyful shouting. He who goes to and fro weeping, carrying his bag of seed, shall indeed come again with a shout of joy, bringing his sheaves with him."

God uses our tears as fertilizer that will produce an eternal crop, an inexpressible joy. So hold on. God is watching you, and He knows and understands all that you are going through. Remember, the payoff, the ultimate reward, is in heaven.

WHERE ARE YOU GOING?

This brings me to the second decision we must make when we are visited with hard times. As we journey through this life, *we must keep our eyes on where we are going.*

When I was growing up, sometimes I would lose my focus. Perhaps my grades weren't as good as they should have been. Or I would misbehave and get into some trouble, and I would have to face my father. More often than not, Pop would give me "the speech." It went something like this: "Boy, do you know *why* your mother and I are doing the best we can to raise you and your sisters? Because we see what you can be. And I'm not going to put up with you doing less than you ought to do. Growing up, I didn't have near the opportunities that you have. You need to do something about them. You need to start acting like you're going somewhere!"

Pop was trying to help me see something that at the time I didn't understand or appreciate. He was calling me to step up and pursue my destiny—to act like I knew where I was going.

Karen and I sought to teach the same lesson to our children. As they were growing up, we paid attention to the passions they began developing as they went through their teenage years. Each one eventually developed a certain bent, a calling, and we would encourage them to follow that passion no matter what obstacles came in their way.

OUR STRENGTH TO ENDURE IS FOUND IN OUR VISION FOR OUR DESTINY.

For example, our youngest daughter, Holly, has always wanted to be a physician. And when we saw that this was more than just a passing interest, we began to encourage her. But we also wanted her to have a realistic picture of what it was going to take to fulfill her dream. Between her desire and the fulfillment is a long, hard, challenging road. We're talking eight long years of intense collegiate training and preparation. But if that is the vision, the dream that God has placed in her heart, then it is worth the sacrifice. And what will keep her going is a clear picture of the finished product. The hassles, hurdles, and setbacks will be all worth it when she reaches her goal.

Our ultimate goal is eternal life with Christ. We are to focus on what will last forever, the eternal. And when we do, we see the suffering and hardships we face here on earth in a new way. We see that this world only offers temporary hope and transient solutions. There's nothing lasting in anything that is not lodged in the eternal.

I am growing increasingly uncomfortable and weary of the "feather-light" Christianity that is becoming popular these days. We're told not to talk too much about hell because it will offend people, and don't talk too much about heaven because it doesn't relate to where people are. So we talk mainly about how the Bible can help improve our lives—how to raise children, how to be a better husband or wife, how to be a leader, how to settle disputes and arguments. Of course nothing is wrong with these messages, and I often speak on these subjects myself. But I fear that too much emphasis on these how-to themes can subtly lead us to focus too much on this world. We begin looking at the Christian life as a sort of members-only club that others can join so they can experience a cool, exciting, and fun life.

But we are not called to build our hope in this world. We are pilgrims, sojourners on a journey to a different place, and this world is a pitiful, shoddy substitute for where we are going. We are pilgrims *moving through this life.* This temporal life does not have what we need to sustain us during hard times. Our strength to endure is found in our vision for our destiny.

Hebrews 11:13–16 teaches us that enduring faith is lodged in that vision of our eternal destiny. Read this passage and meditate on the words for a few moments. Let God pour

His encouragement into your heart and soul. It starts with a reference to heroes of the Old Testament:

All these [saints] died in faith, without receiving the promises, but having seen them and having welcomed them from a distance, and having confessed that they were strangers and exiles on the earth. For those who say such things make it clear that they are seeking a country of their own. And indeed if they had been thinking of that country from which they went out, they would have had opportunity to return. But as it is, they desire a better country, that is a heavenly one. Therefore God is not ashamed to be called their God; for He has prepared a city for them.

The writer of Hebrews succinctly captures the motivation of godly pilgrims. The people he describes had a clear, compelling vision of their eternal home. They knew we are "strangers and exiles" on the earth.

In short, we don't have much in common with this world. We don't really belong here; this world is not our country of origin. We have been temporarily assigned here for a brief moment.

Have you ever thought about what it means to be living in exile, as a stranger in a foreign land? If you've ever spent much time in a foreign country, you know how different it feels. Your accent, traditions, customs, values, and even your diet are often in conflict with this new environment. Your mind drifts back to familiar scenes at home. You can see in your mind the faces of friends and family. You know you don't belong, and you look forward to the familiar sights and sounds and smells of your home. And now imagine what it's like for someone who has been exiled—told never to return.

I realize this illustration breaks down. We're not here in this world because we've been exiled from heaven. No, we're here because something is wrong with this world. It's sort of a reverse exile. When we gave our lives to Christ, God could have immediately taken us to our home. Instead, He gave us the gift of eternal life and placed inside us a sense of destiny, a longing for home. He has kept us here in this "country of exile" to influence others.

When we approach this life as if it is the ultimate payoff, we do irreparable damage to our endurance. We expect something that this world cannot deliver. The pilgrims in Hebrews 11 understood this. So they acknowledged and accepted the temporary, transient nature of this life and kept moving toward their destiny, toward a perfect place with a perfect Savior. That vision and that hope pulled them through and gave them the strength to keep walking through the "valley of the shadow of death" (Psalm 23:4). And it will do the same for us if we will embrace the reality that we are strangers and exiles down here.

At this point I need to add that, yes, God wants us to enjoy this life! Just as those living temporarily in another country enjoy their lives and make the best of their experience, we should savor the pleasures of this life. We laugh, we savor time with family and friends, we value and appreciate the beauty of this world and the experiences along the journey. Much like a family vacation, we take time to enjoy the sights and scenery along the way. But we have to keep moving because we're going somewhere.

Could it be that you have been drained of your spiritual strength and energy because you have taken your sights off where you are going?

"It Was Worth It All!"

Finally, if we're going to maintain the strength to endure the suffering and adversity along this journey, we need to *stay focused on a person, Jesus Christ.*

Throughout Hebrews 11, the writer gives us biographical snapshots of men and women of God, pilgrims who despite adversity and challenges kept moving. They tapped into their destiny for the motivation they needed. Then the author closes out this incredible section of Scripture by pointing us to our ultimate source of strength and motivation.

Look closely at these words from Hebrews 12:1–3:

> *Therefore, since we have so great a cloud of witnesses surrounding us, let us also lay aside every encumbrance, and the sin which so easily entangles us, and let us run with endurance the race that is set before us, fixing our eyes on Jesus, the author and perfecter of faith, who for the joy set before Him endured the cross, despising the shame, and has sat down at the right hand of the throne of God. For consider Him who has endured such hostility by sinners against Himself, so that you may not grow weary and lose heart.*

It is appropriate that the writer of Hebrews speaks of our need to "run the race with endurance." Any distance runner knows about pain. And one of the tricks to enduring pain and hardship is to keep your mind on your goal.

The "cloud of witnesses" here is the believers described in chapter 11—those who have gone on before us and finished the race. They are in the very presence of God. They endured, and they are safely home. But as great as these men and women were, they were imperfect men and women. They endured difficulties, pain, suffering. Some were even martyred for their faithfulness.

Nobody, however, has ever experienced the pain and suffering of our Savior. And I'm not just talking about the horrors of crucifixion. There have been thousands who have been crucified, and in that respect there was nothing particularly unique about death on the cross.

Awful, brutal, and painful? Yes.

Unusual? No. It was the Romans' preferred method of capital punishment.

The suffering of our Savior's cross, however, was beyond anything any human has experienced or ever will experience. The sins of the world were placed upon Him. He died in our place (2 Corinthians 5:21; 1 John 2:2). Jesus, driven by love, willingly submitted Himself to the excruciating agony of the cross (John 15:13; John 10:14–18). And Hebrews 12:2 tells us the reason why He endured such unimaginable suffering: "For the joy set before Him."

What was this joy? Certainly not the experience of the cross; Jesus referred to that as a bitter cup from which He did not want to drink (Matthew 26:39). No, He knew what His future held. He knew there was an empty chair that belonged to Him at the right hand of the throne of God.

Read Hebrews 12:3 again. "For consider Him who has endured such hostility by sinners against Himself *so that you may not grow weary and lose heart."* When you feel like quitting . . . when you are overwhelmed . . . when the tears of pain and sorrow and disappointment cascade down your cheeks—find a quiet place and pour out your heart to God. Place your burdens at the foot of the cross. Then, consider what Jesus endured for you, and how He was able to find joy in the midst of affliction and suffering.

Take a sip from this cup of certainty. Heaven is our home. It's where we belong. We will be rewarded, and when we leave this place of exile and see our Savior face-to-face, we will say, "It was worth it all!"

In the meantime, keep your eyes on Jesus. He is called the "author and perfecter [completer] of [our] faith." Our Savior is omnipresent; He is not only seated at the right hand of His

Father, but He also is with us right now! He has saved us, and He is sustaining us today. He is the source of our strength, and He will usher us into His presence. He is alive. He has given us His Word, and His Spirit, and access to riches in heaven that we can tap into at this very moment through prayer.

We are indeed going home. But He has given us plenty of fuel for the journey. What amazing love!

SOON AND VERY SOON

Soon and very soon, we are going to see the King
Hallelujah! Hallelujah! We're going to see the King.

No more crying there, we are going to see the King
Hallelujah! Hallelujah! We're going to see the King.

No more dying there, we are going to see the King
Hallelujah! Hallelujah! We're going to see the King.

Notes

1. C. J. Mahaney with Kevin Meath, *The Cross Centered Life* (Sisters, Ore.: Multnomah, 2002), 42.

2. Bill Bright, *Come Help Change the World* (Old Tappan, N.J.: Revell, 1970), 25.

3. Bill Bright, *The Journey Home* (Nashville: Nelson, 2004), 11.

4. George M. Marsden, *Jonathan Edwards: A Life* (New Haven, Conn.: Yale University Press, 2003), 133.

5. Corrie ten Boom with Jamie Buckingham, *Tramp for the Lord,* (New York: Jove Books, 1978), 45–47

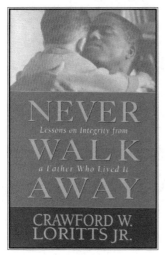

Like countless children, you may have grown up without a strong model of godly manhood. Yet it is not too late to start a new cycle of faithfulness. The potential of your own legacy rests not in the example provided by your earthly dad, but in the hope and promises extended by your Heavenly Father.

Never Walk Away
ISBN: 0-8024-2742-1

Is your faith low on passion? Many Christians struggle at times with a lack of purpose, fulfillment and zeal. But the Christian life was intended to be something else; Christ promised an abundant life to His followers. Many times believers miss that abundance because they have become distracted from the purpose of the Christian life. Includes study guide for individual or small group use.

A Passionate Commitment
ISBN: 0-8024-5246-9

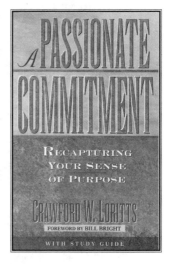

SINCE 1894, Moody Publishers has been dedicated to equip and motivate people to advance the cause of Christ by publishing evangelical Christian literature and other media for all ages, around the world. Because we are a ministry of the Moody Bible Institute of Chicago, a portion of the proceeds from the sale of this book go to train the next generation of Christian leaders.

If we may serve you in any way in your spiritual journey toward understanding Christ and the Christian life, please contact us at www.moodypublishers.com.

"All Scripture is God-breathed and is useful for teaching, rebuking, correcting and training in righteousness, so that the man of God may be thoroughly equipped for every good work."
—2 TIMOTHY 3:16, 17

MOODY
PUBLISHERS

THE NAME YOU CAN TRUST®

FOR A TIME WE CANNOT SEE TEAM

ACQUIRING EDITOR
Greg Thornton

COPY EDITOR
Ali Childers

BACK COVER COPY
Michele Straubel

COVER DESIGN
John Hamilton,
The DesignWorks Group, Inc.
www.thedesignworksgroup.com

COVER PHOTO
Masterfile

INTERIOR DESIGN
BlueFrog Design

PRINTING AND BINDING
Versa Press, Inc.

The typeface for the text of this book is
Centaur MT